RELAXING
Coloring Book for Adult

Vol. 2

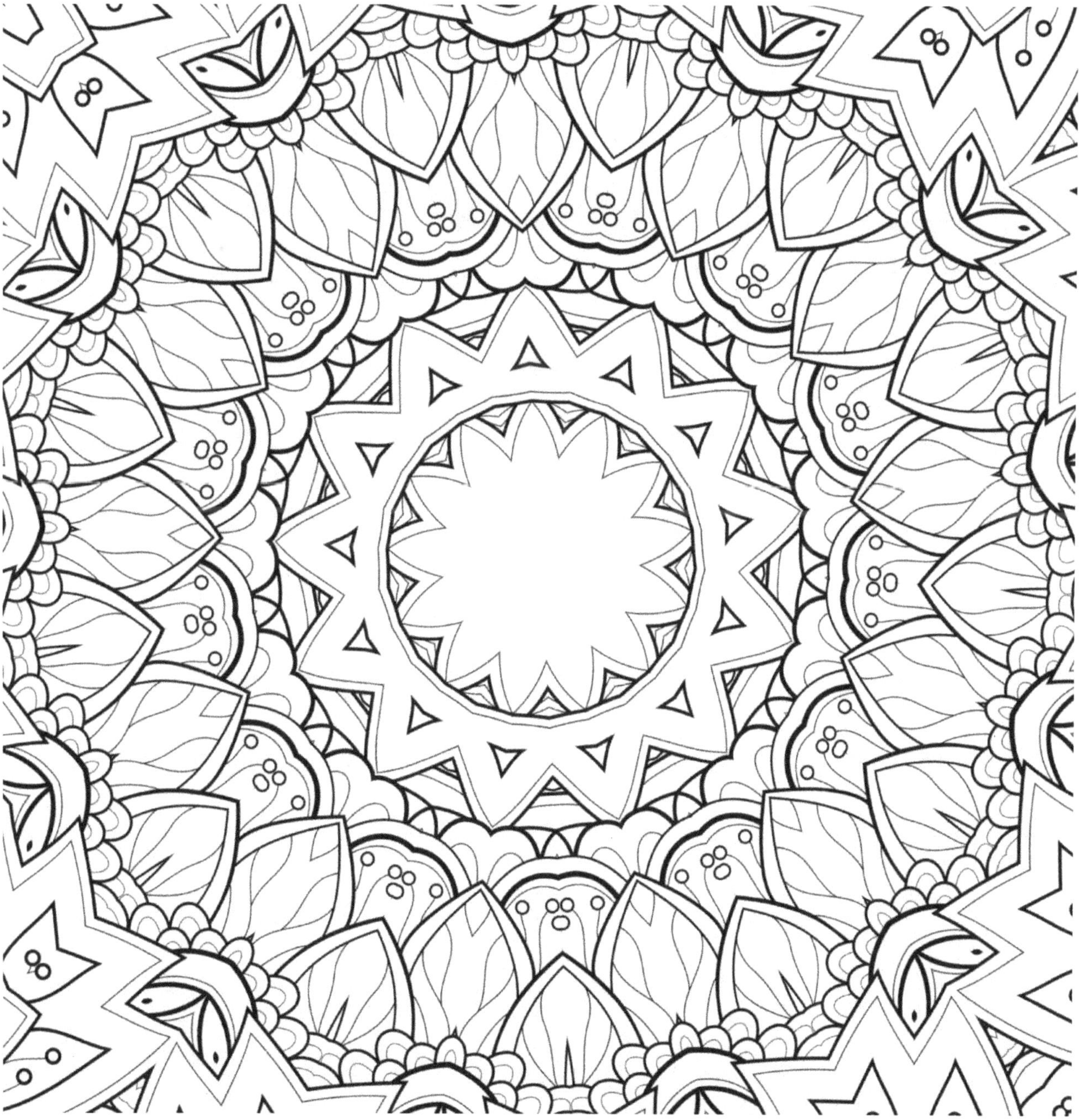

V ART™

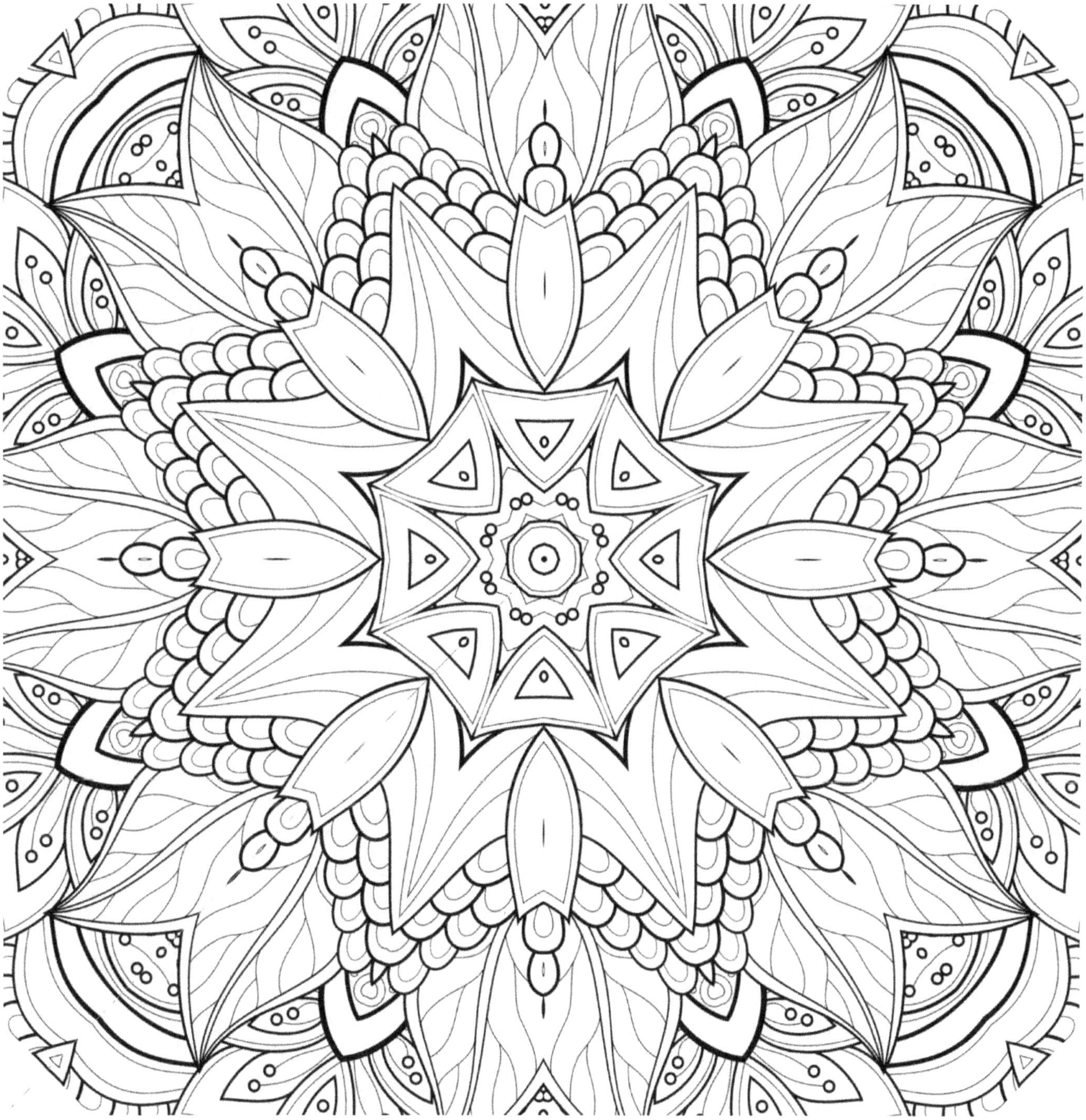

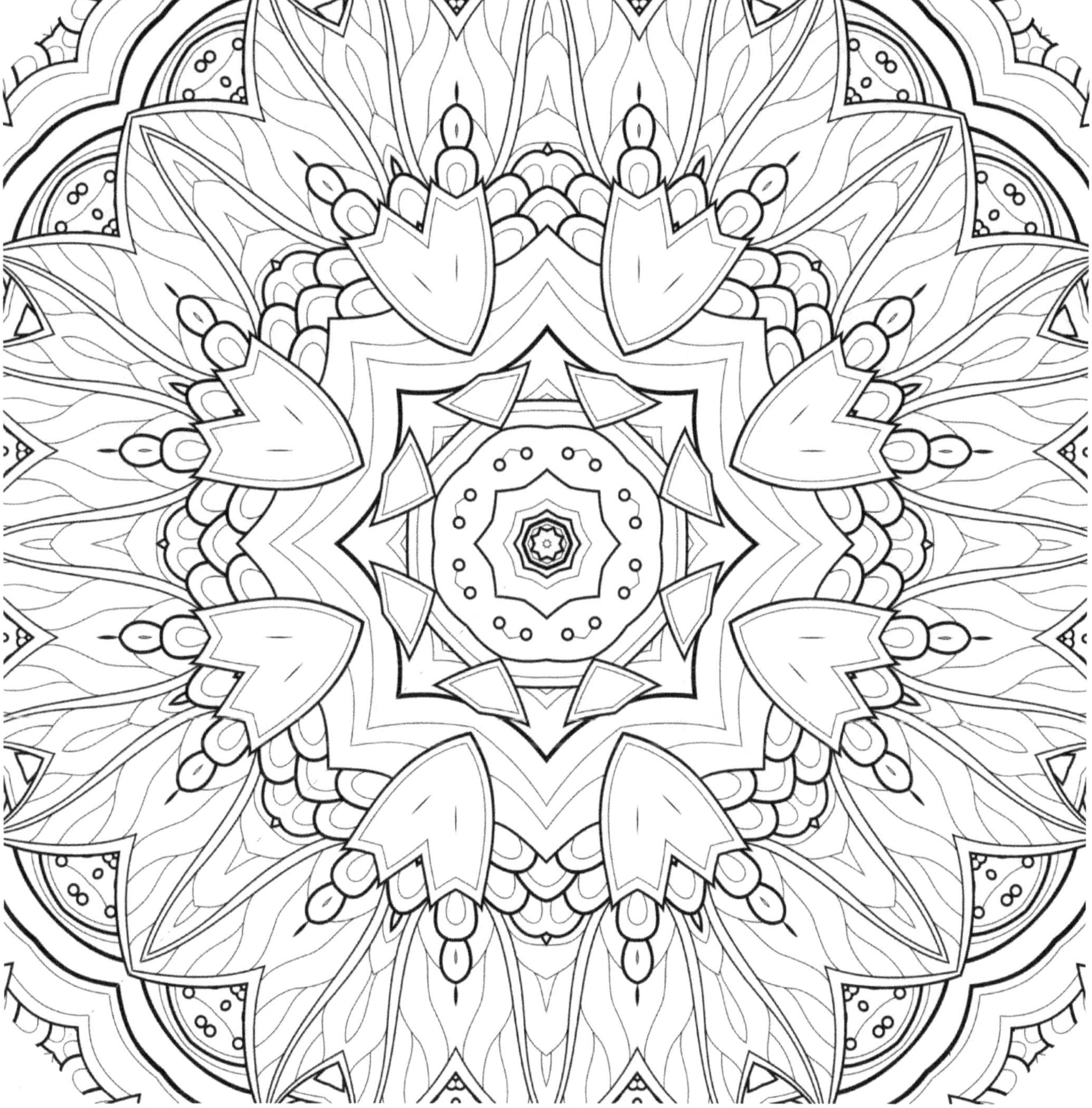

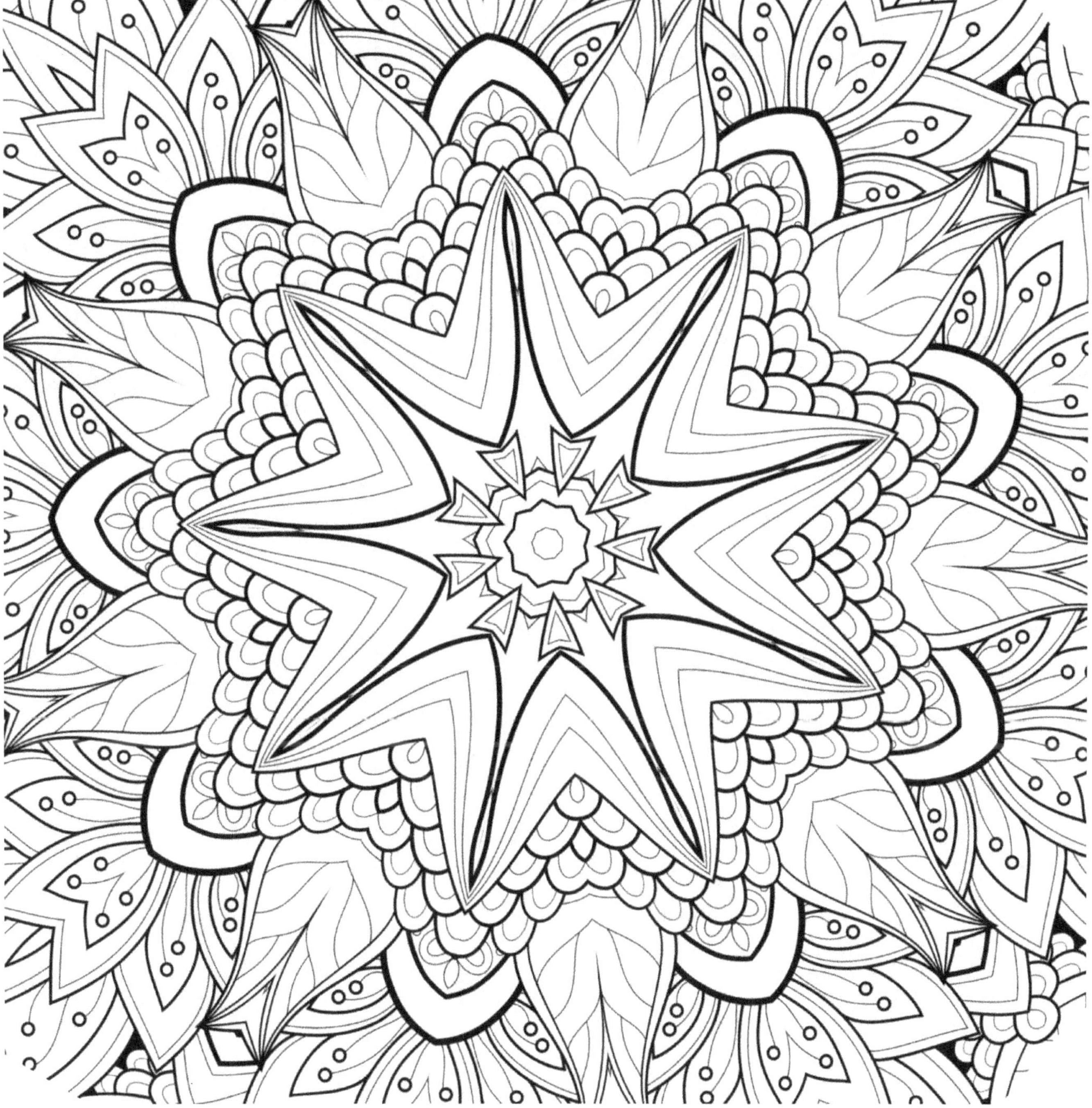

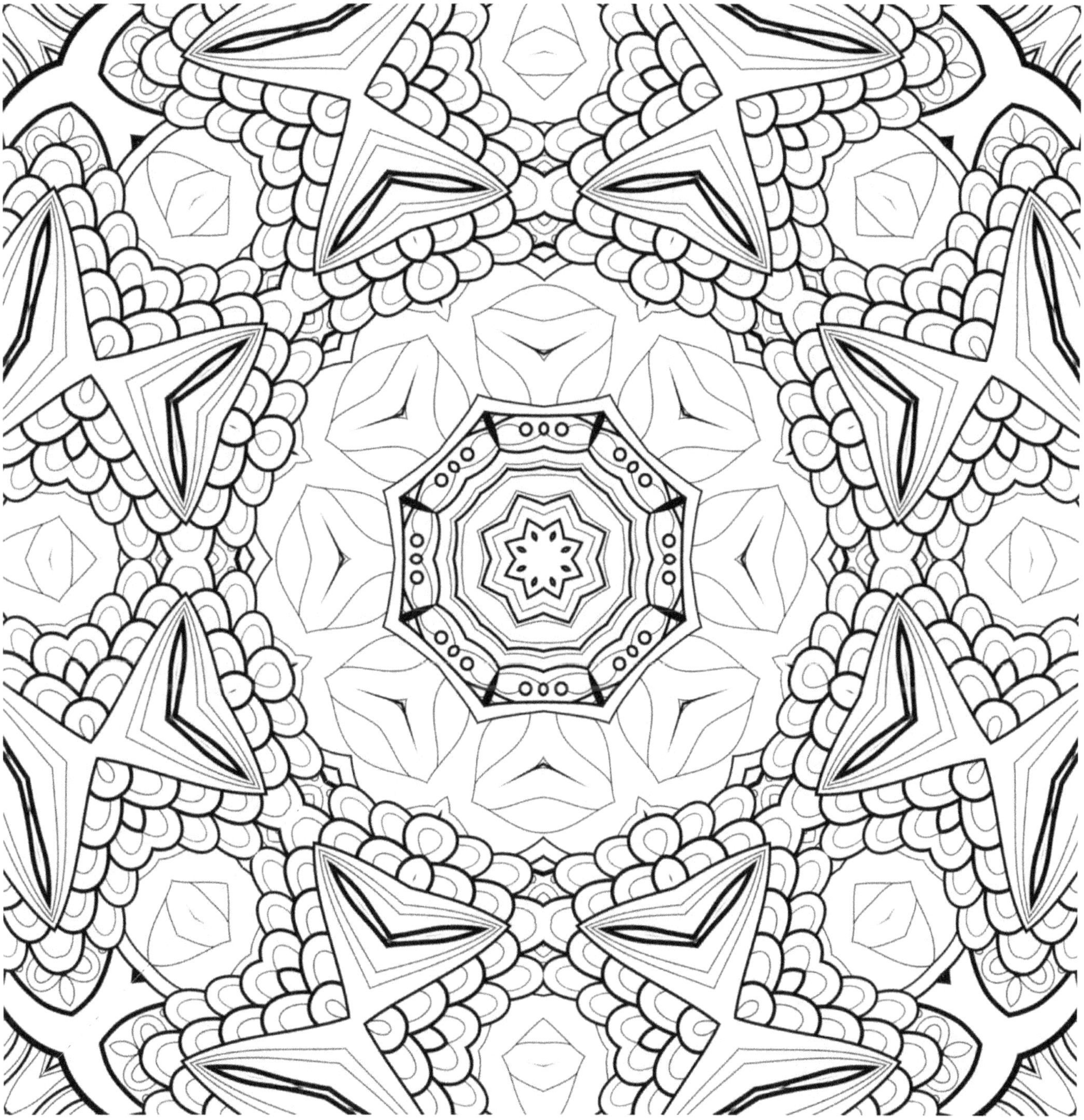

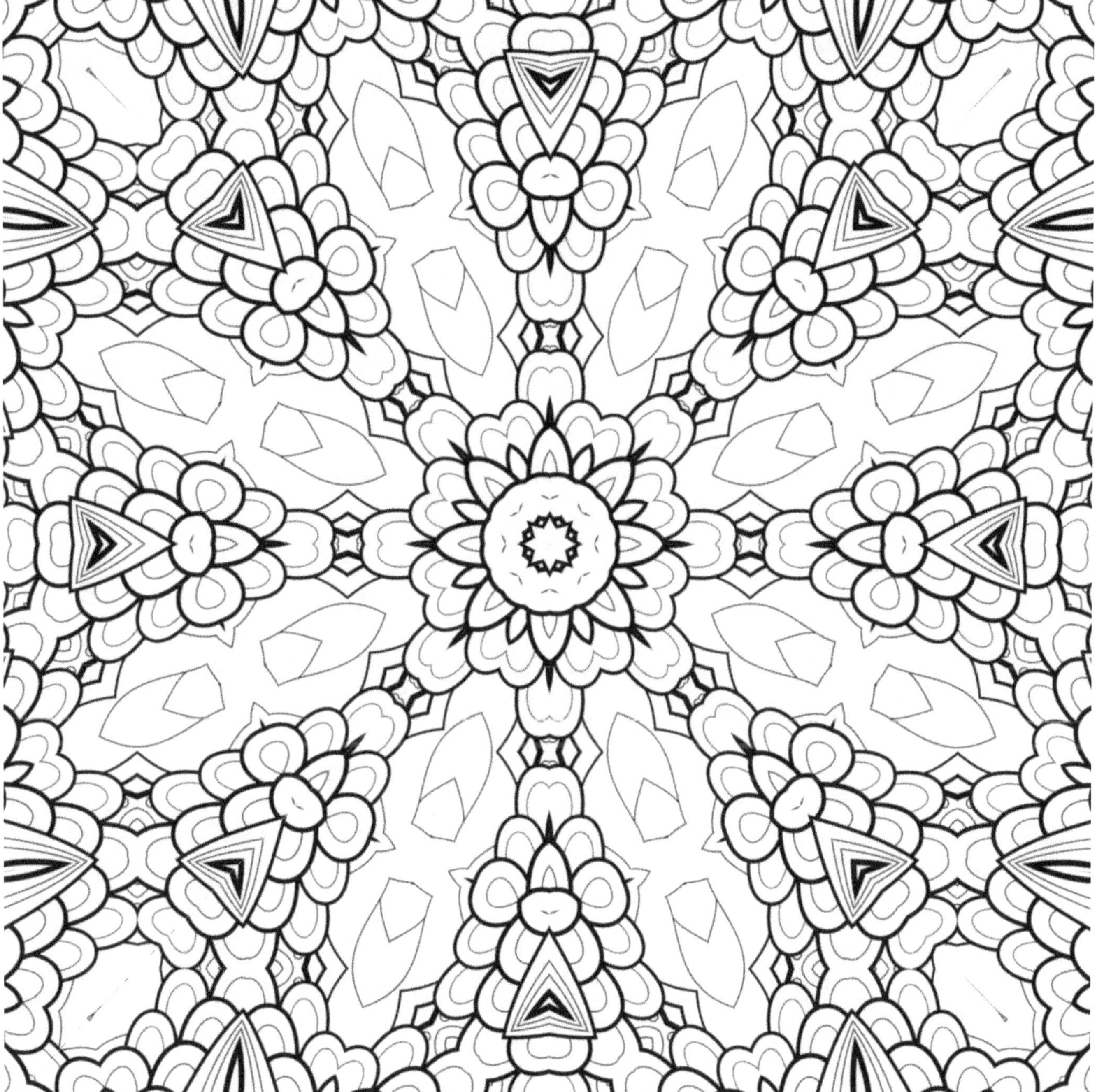

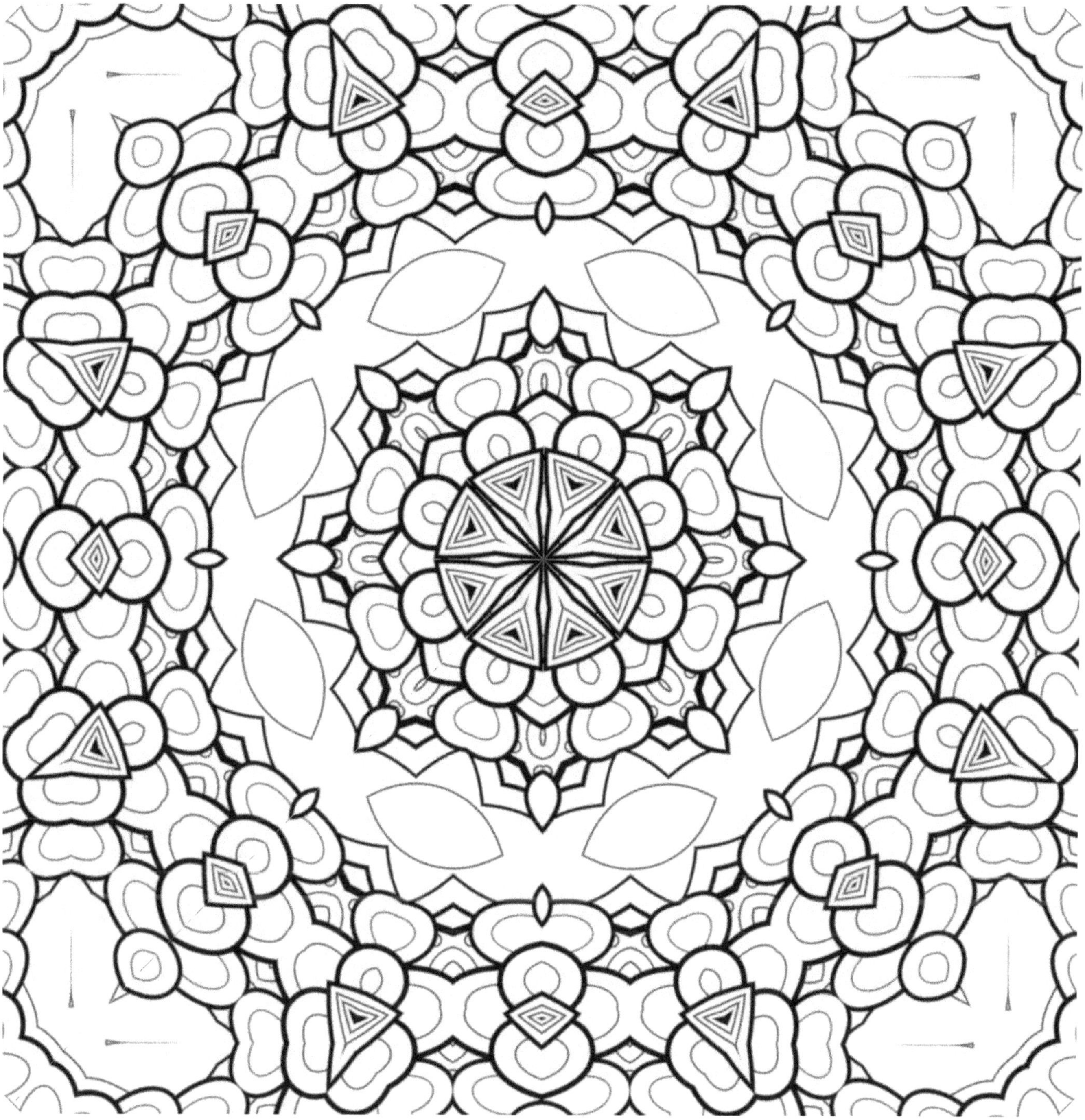

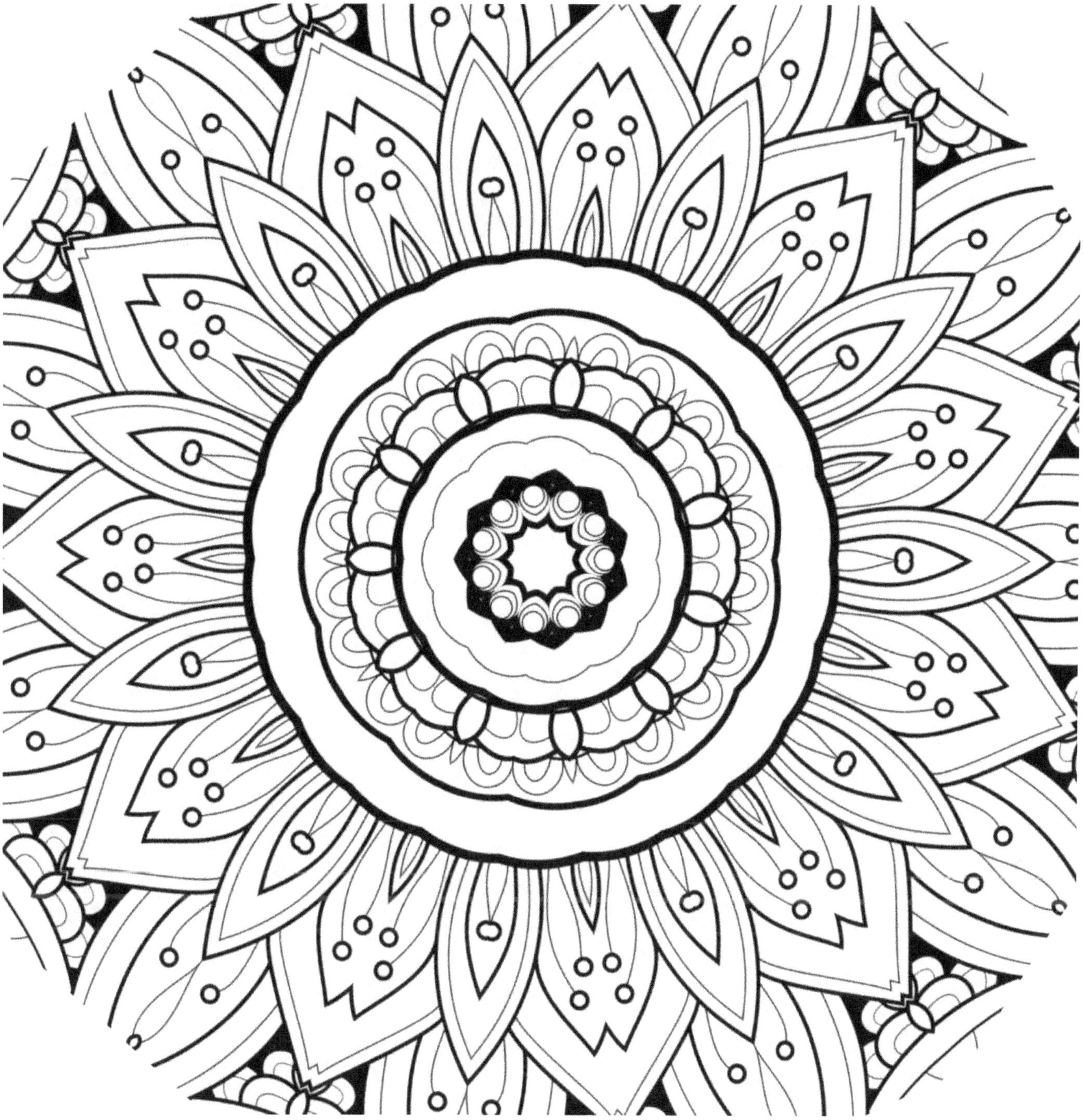

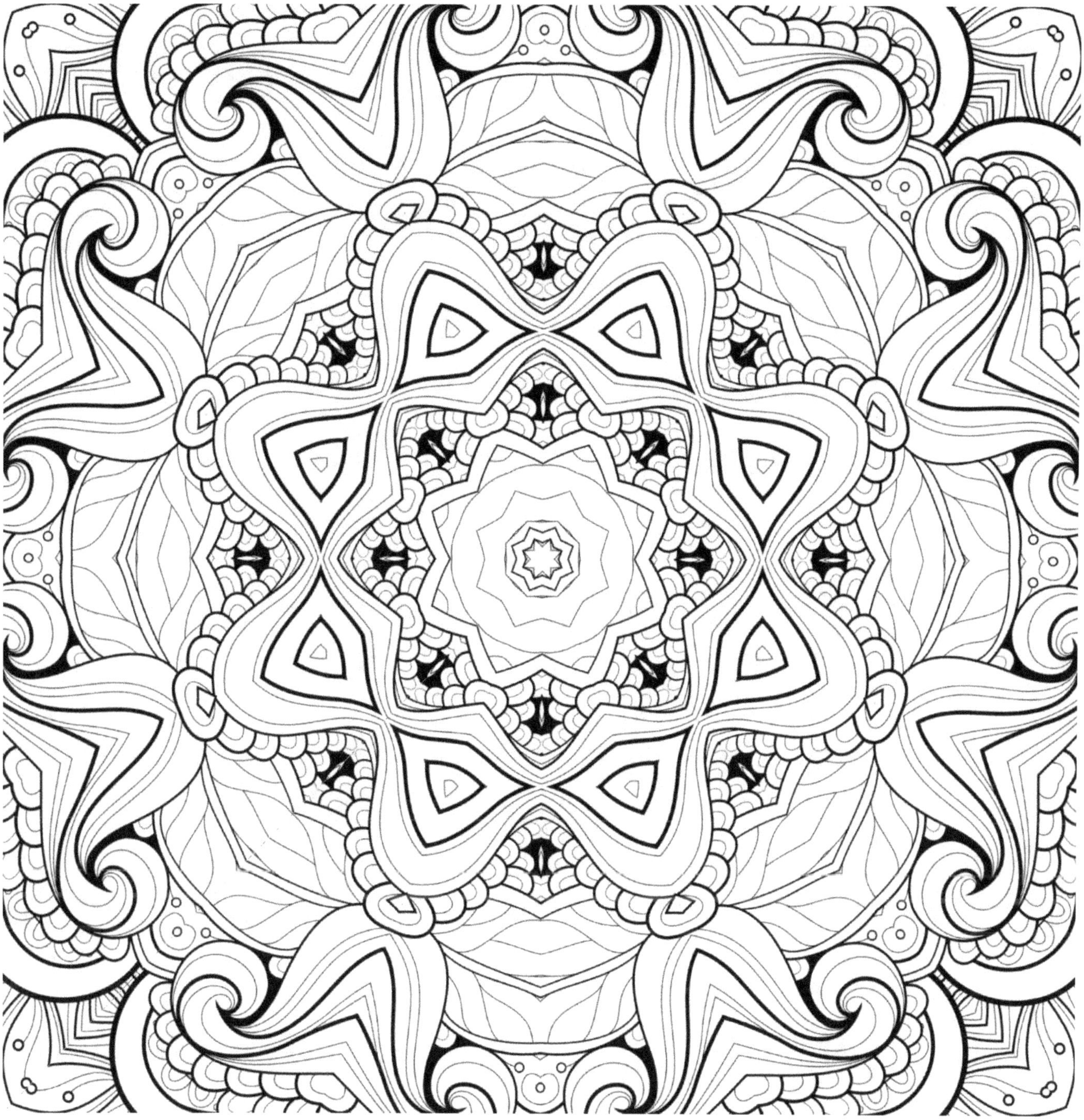

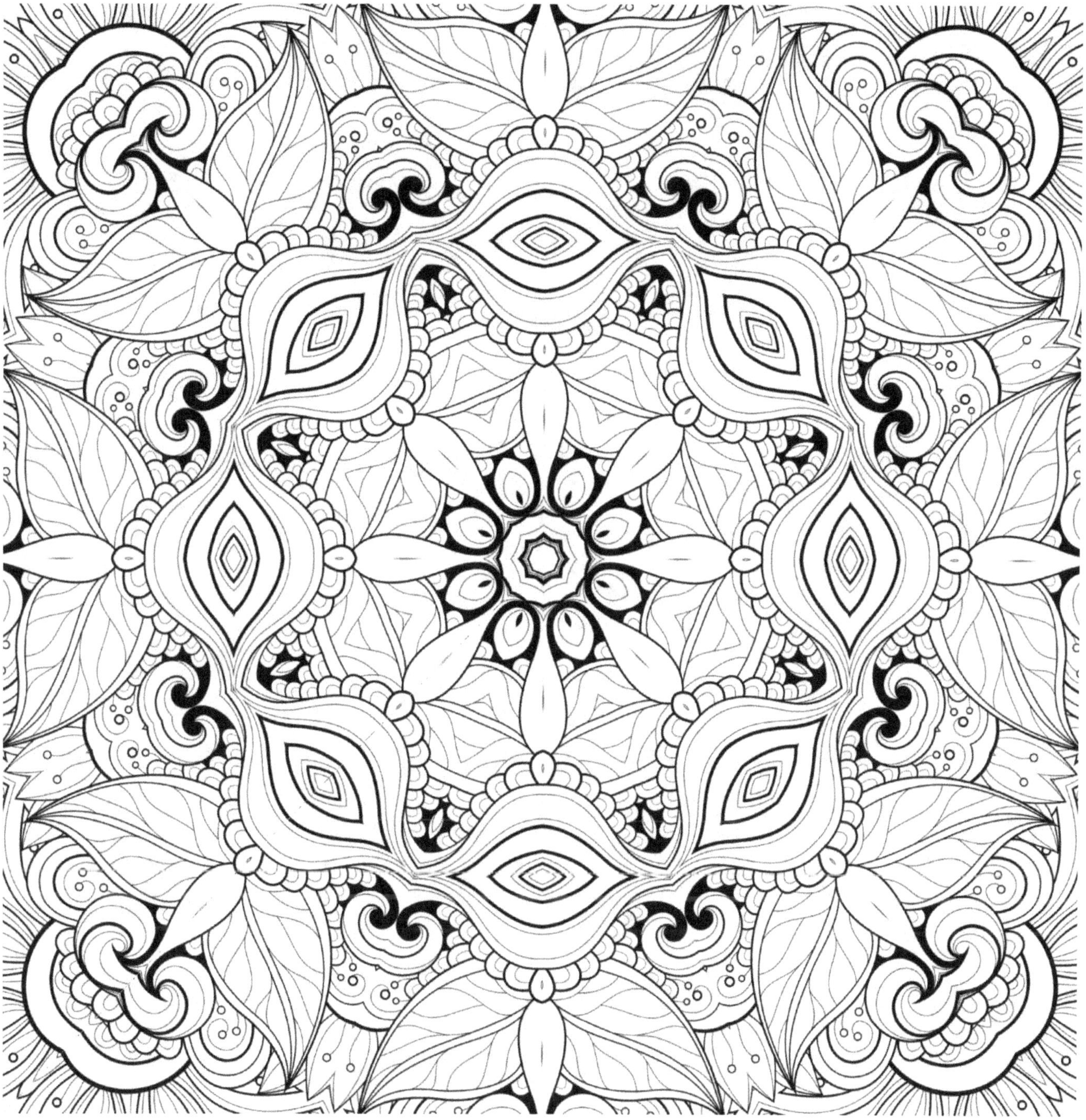

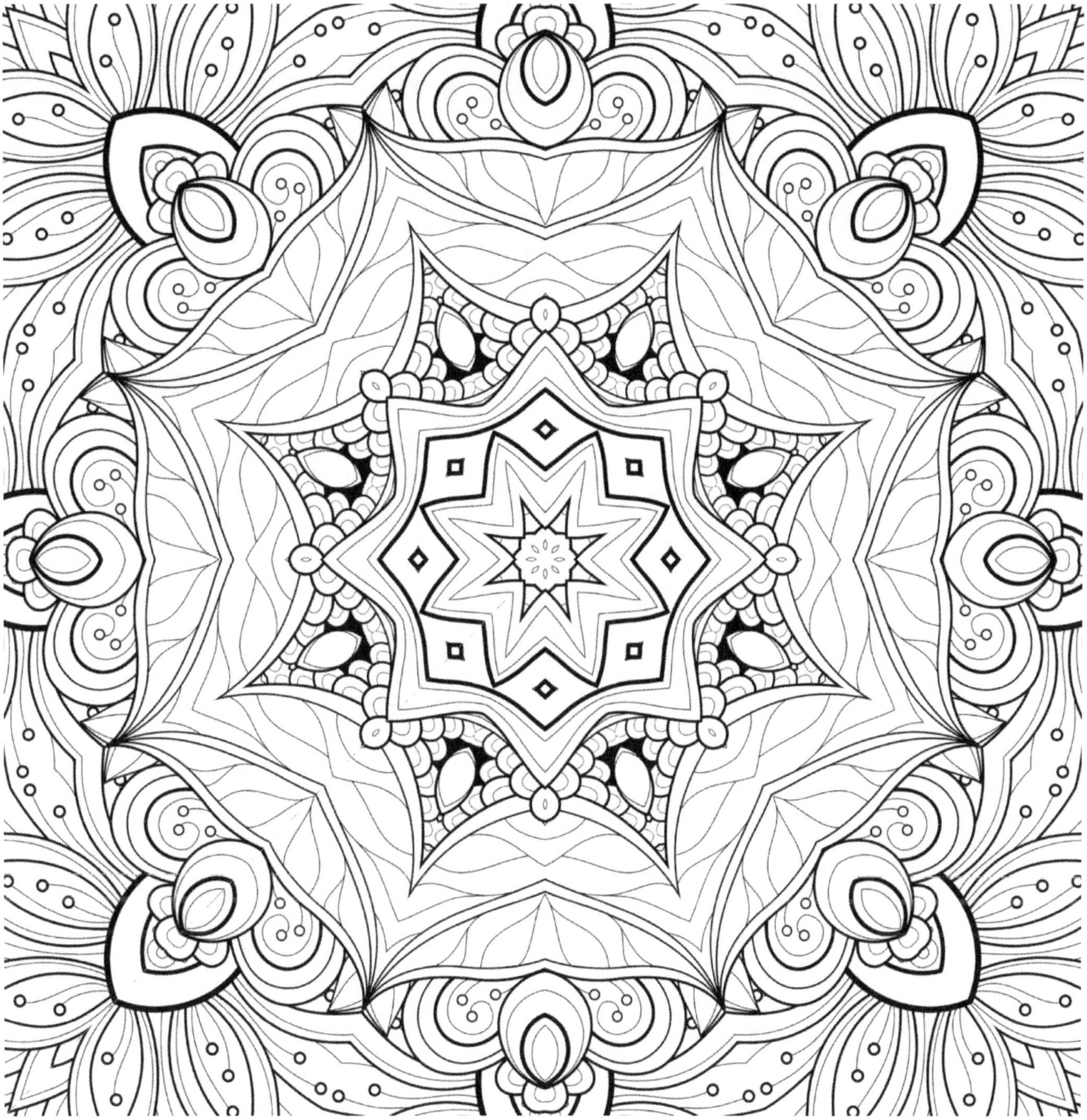

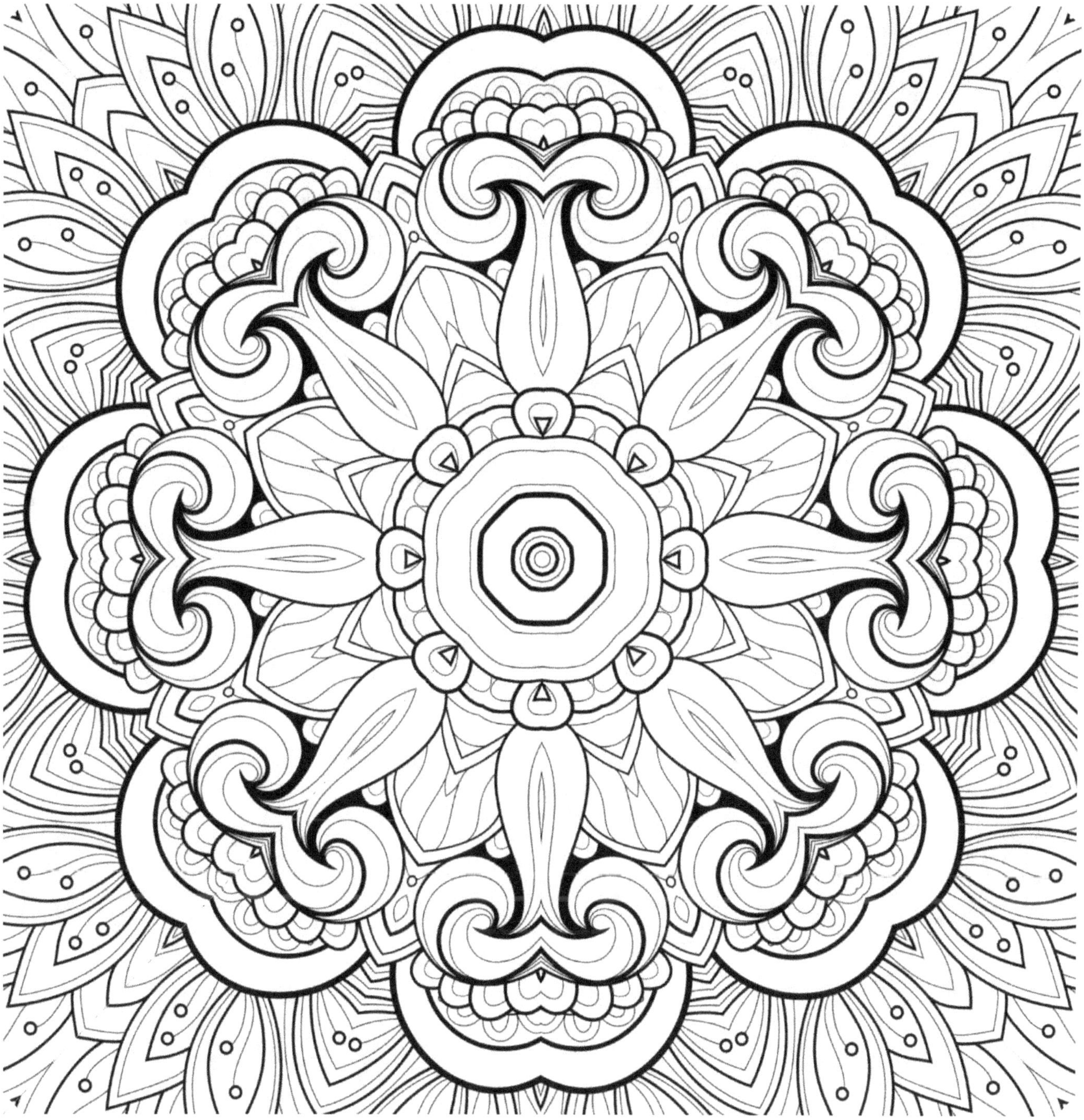

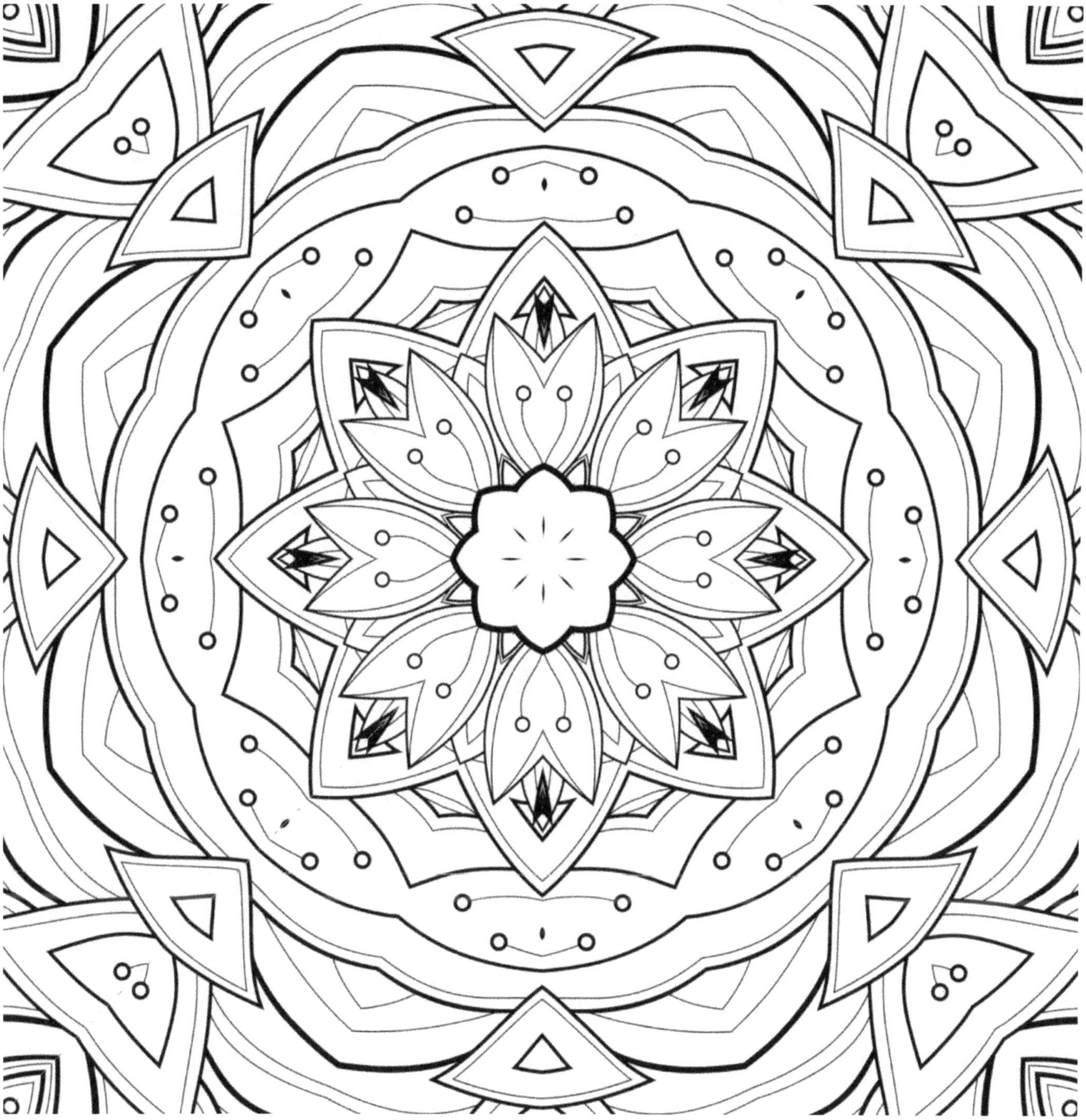

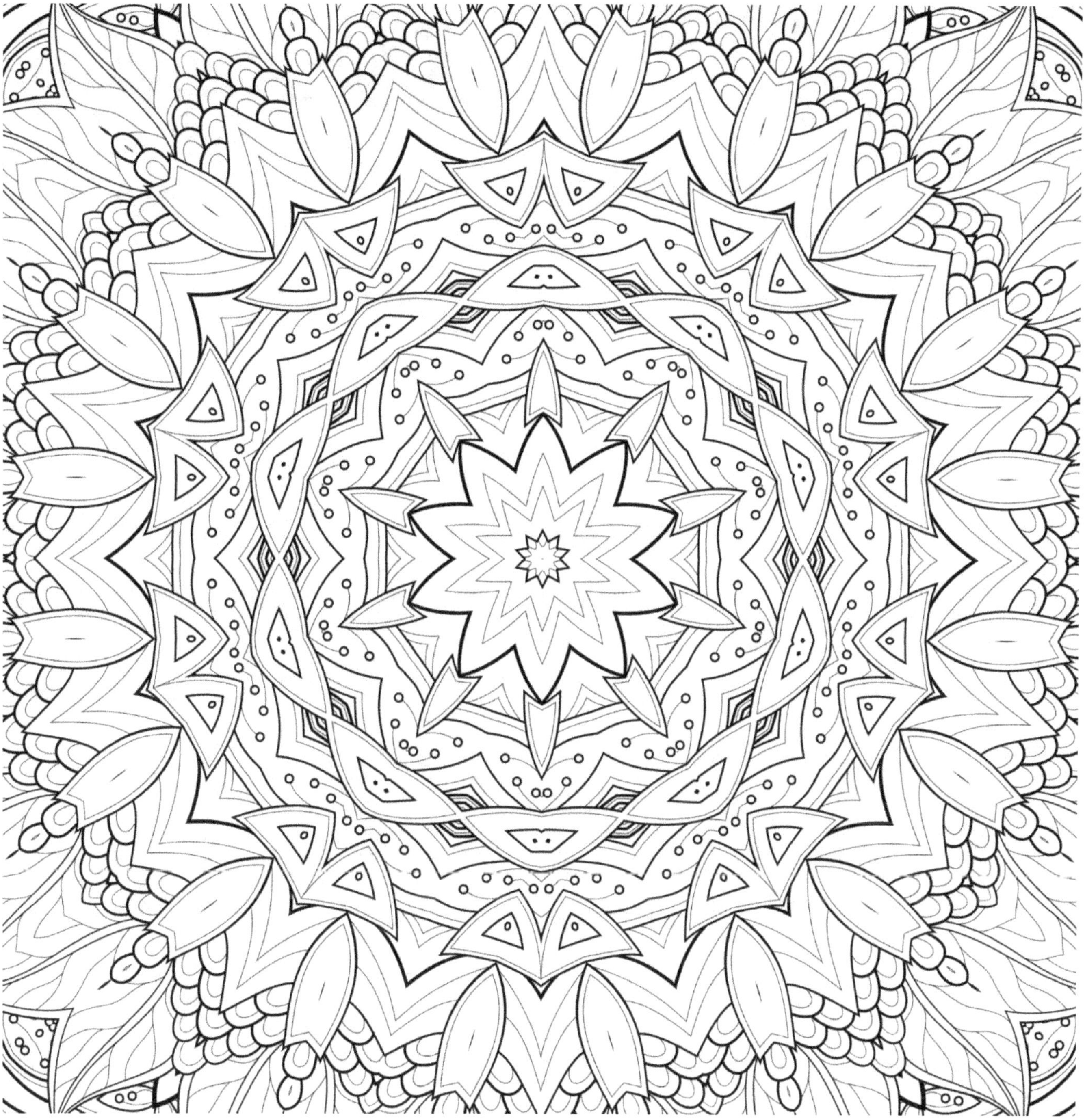

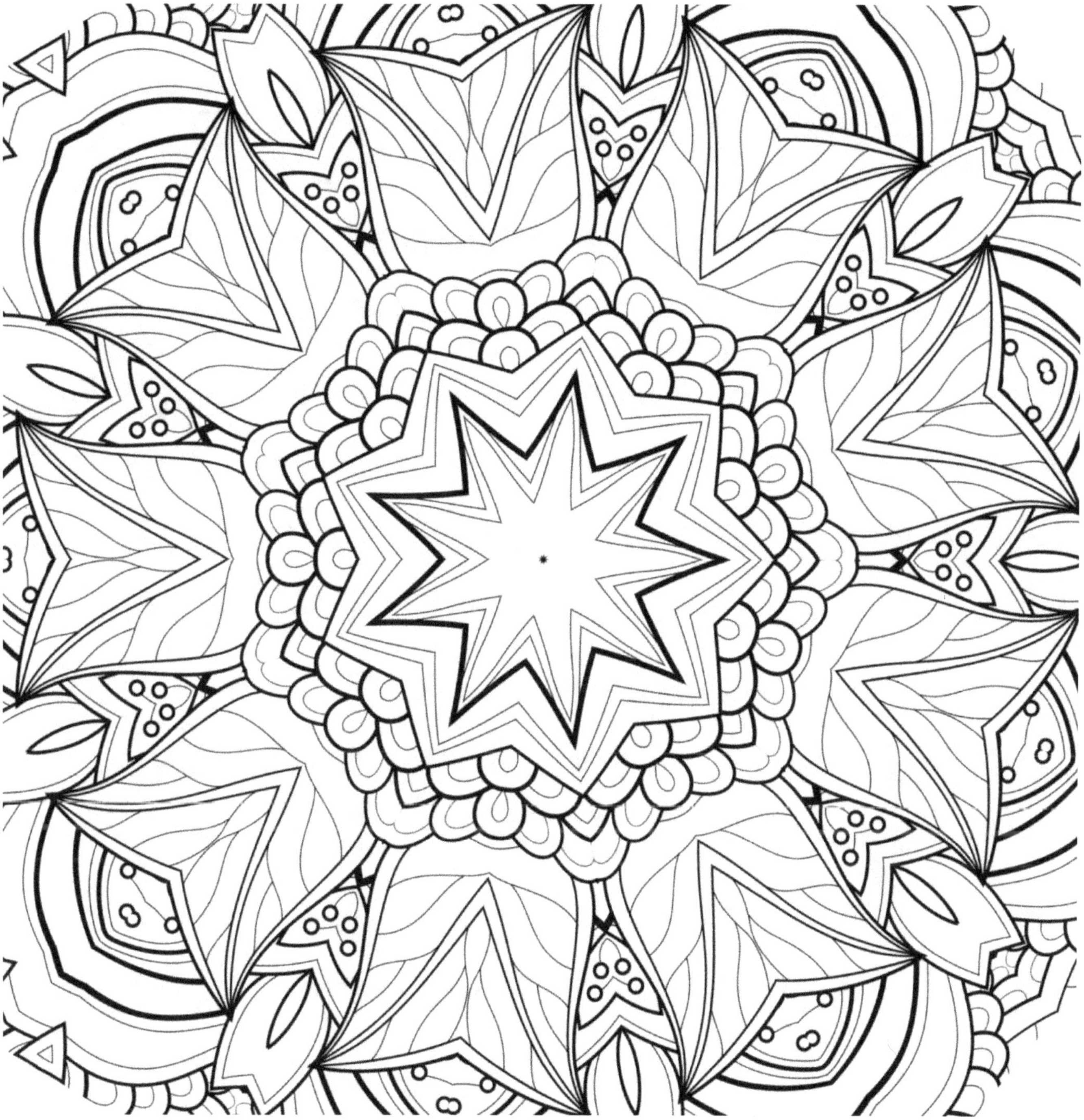

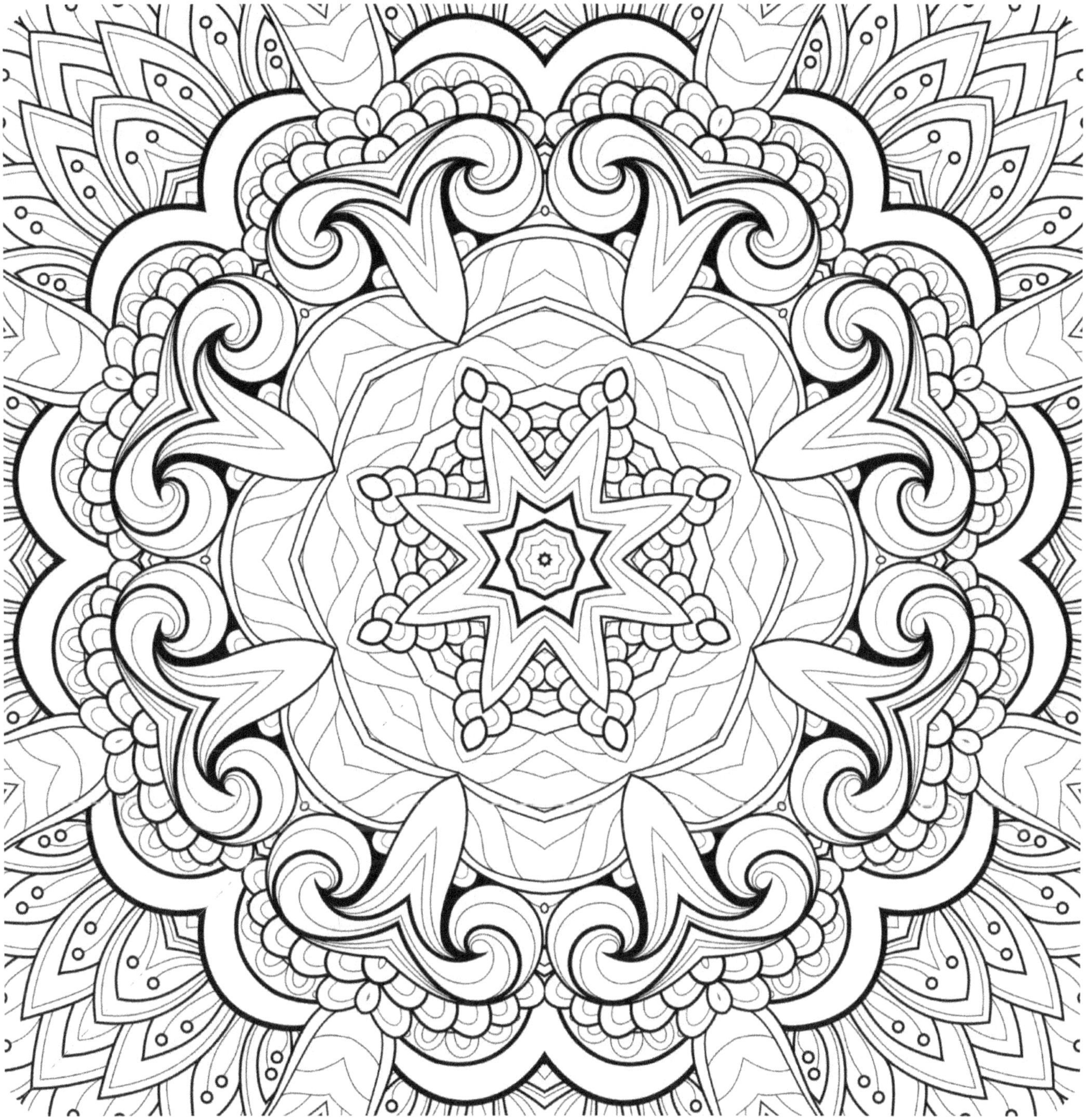

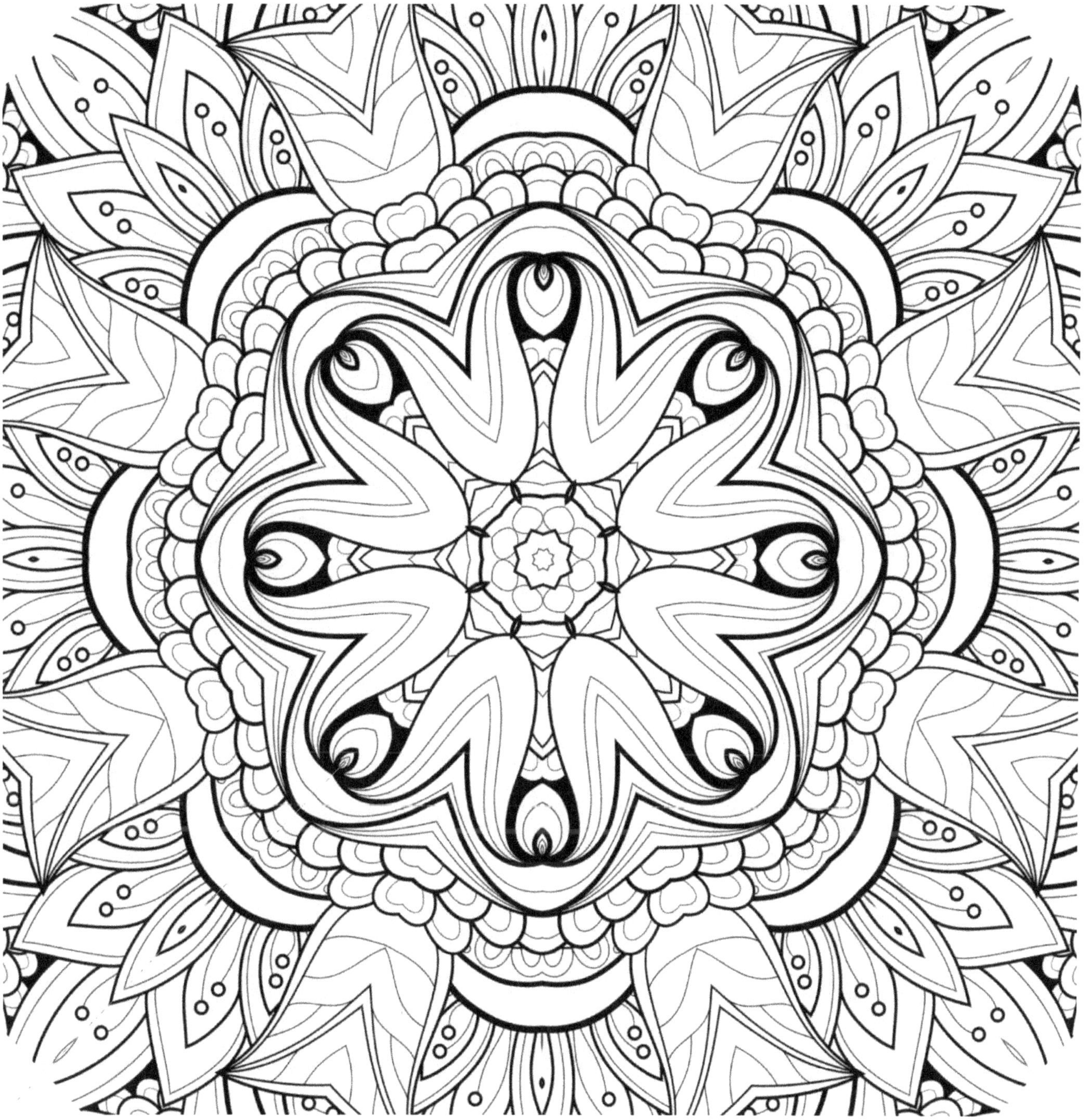

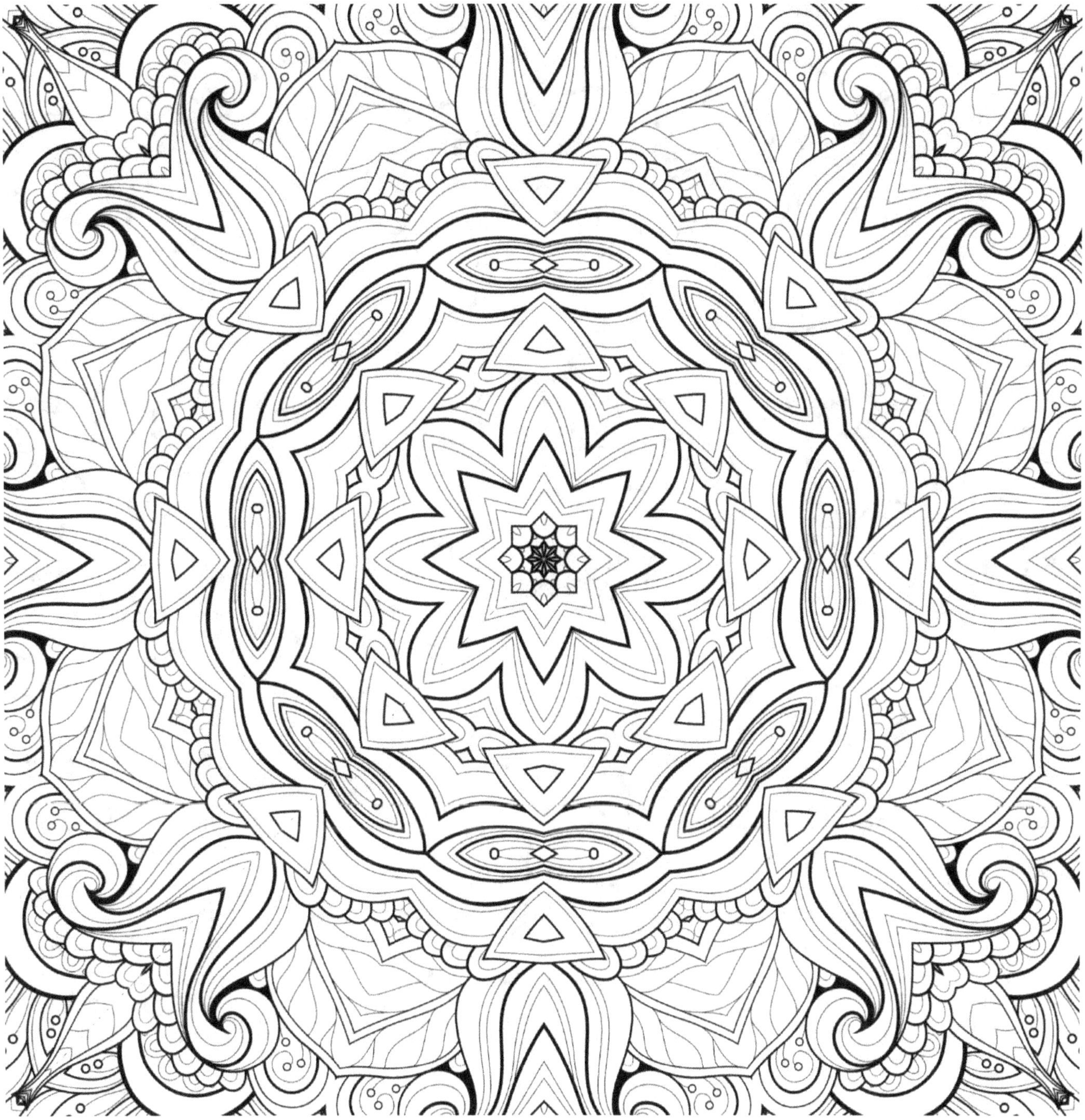

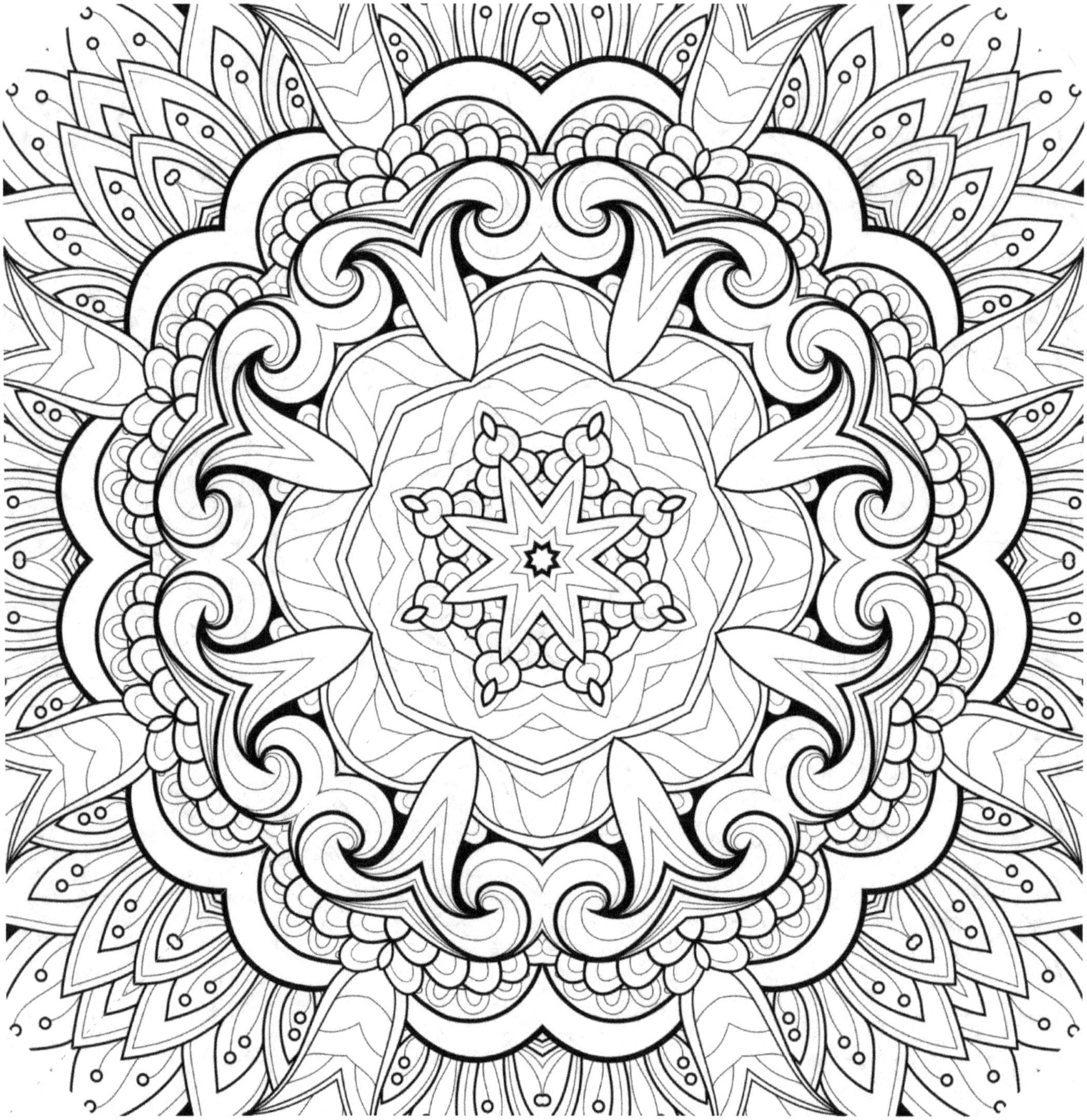

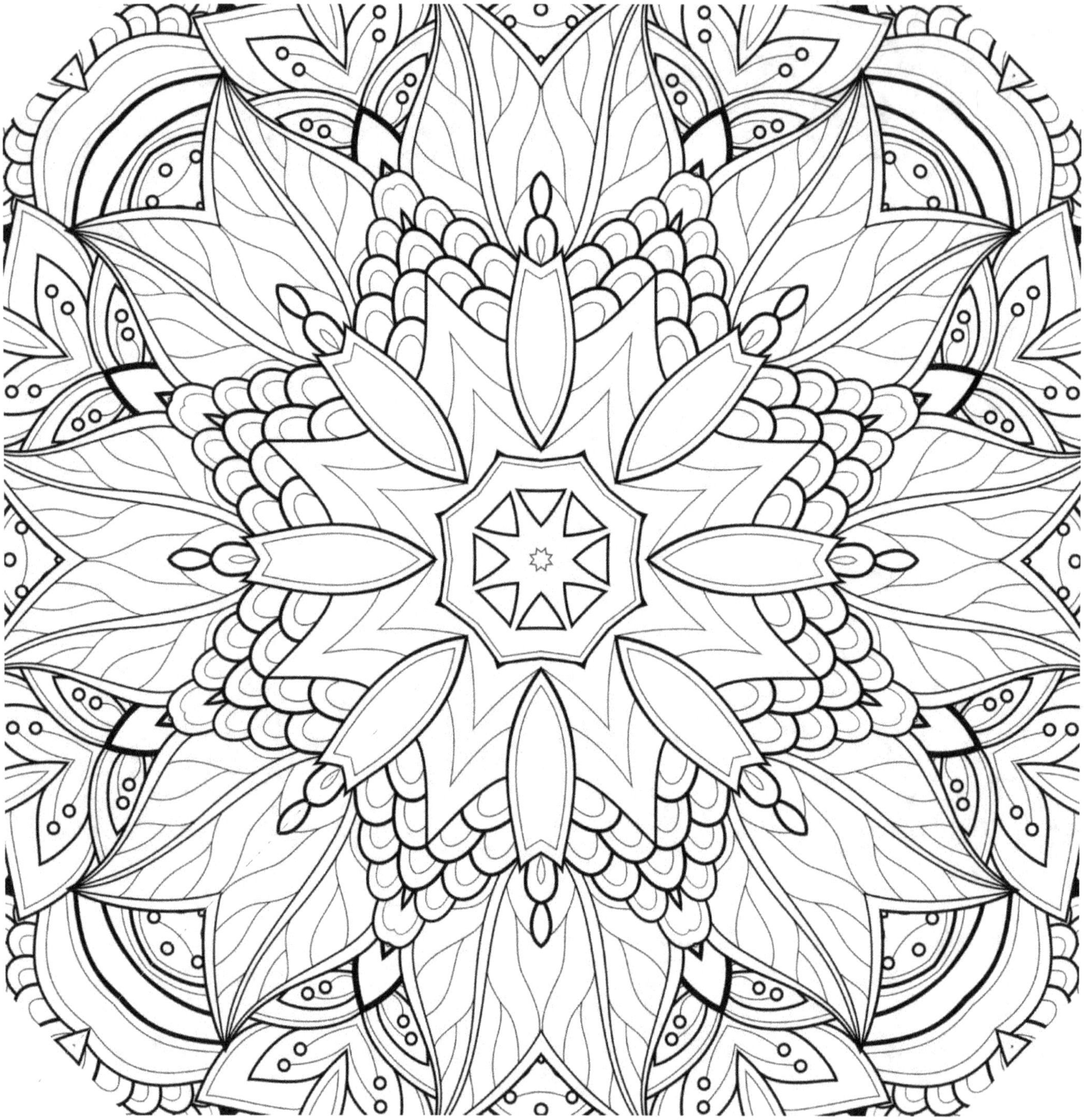

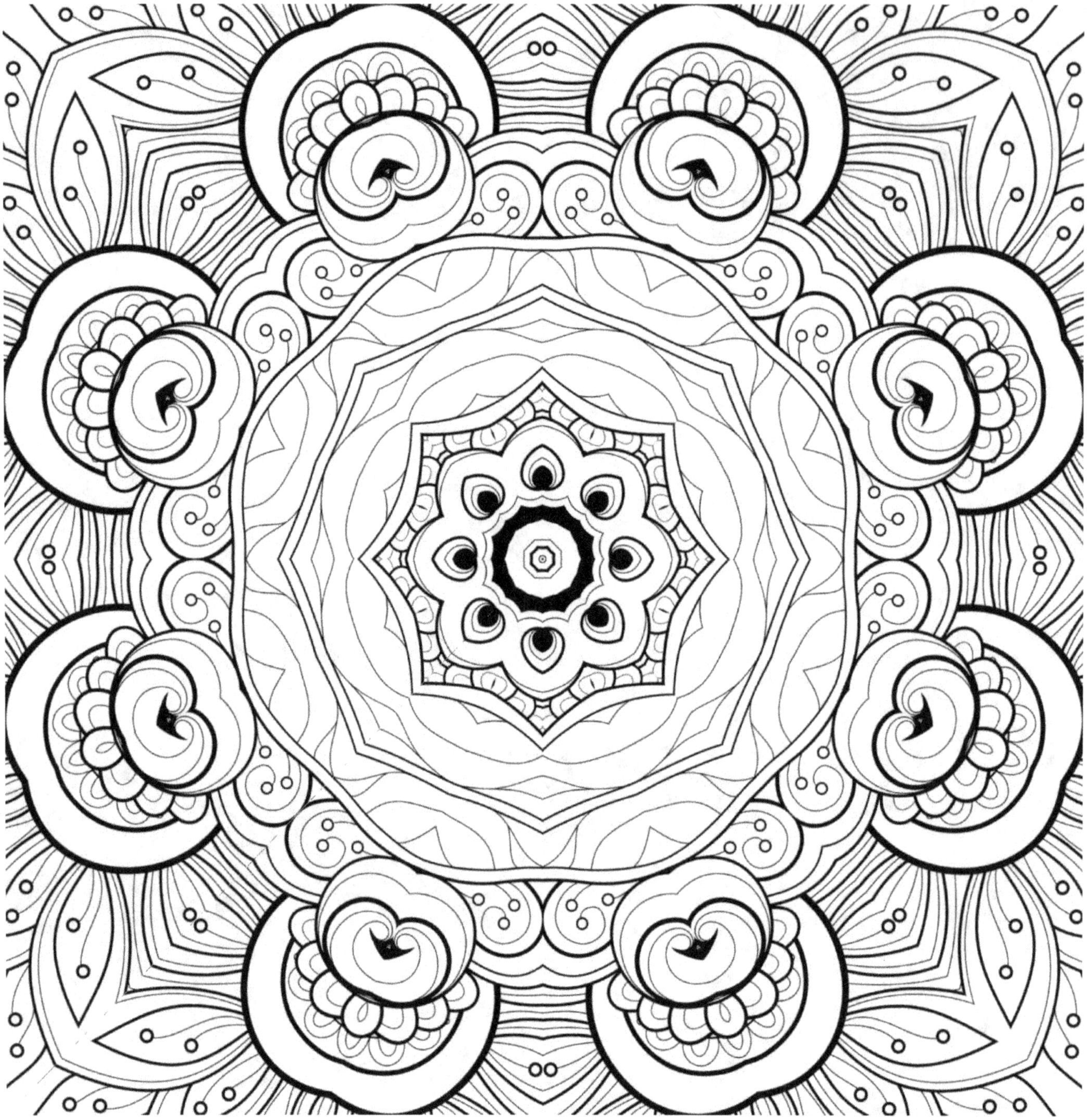

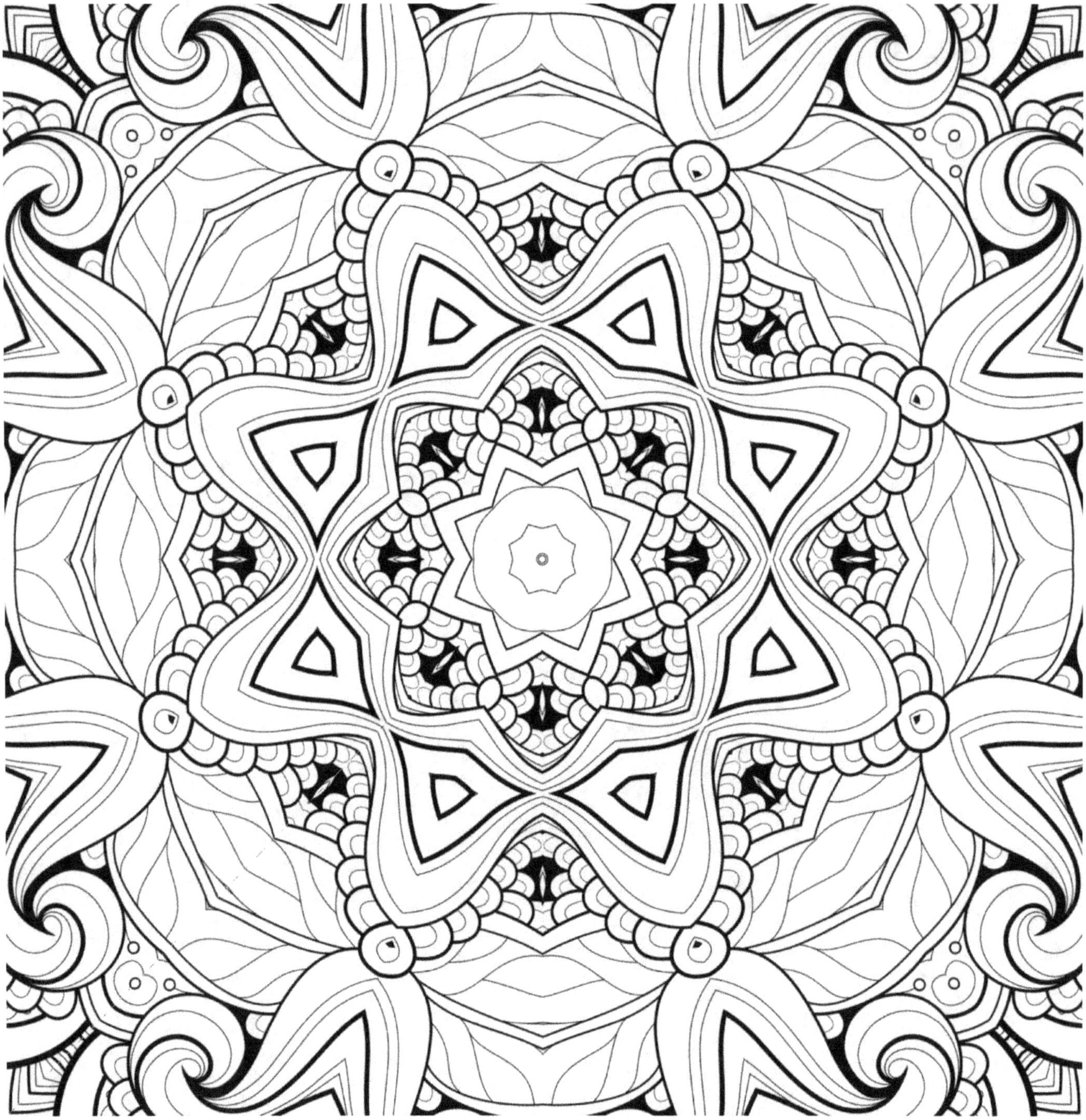

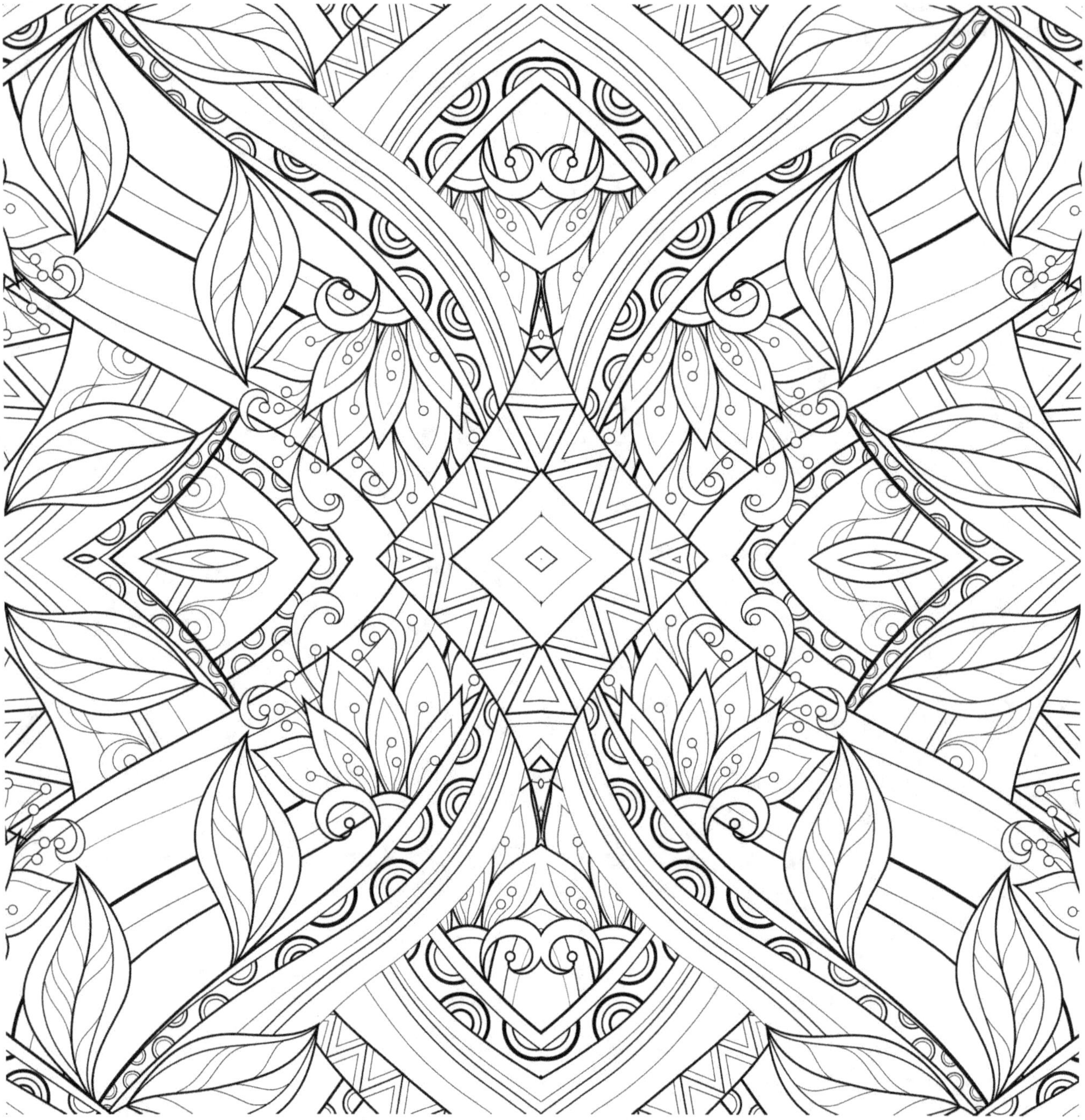

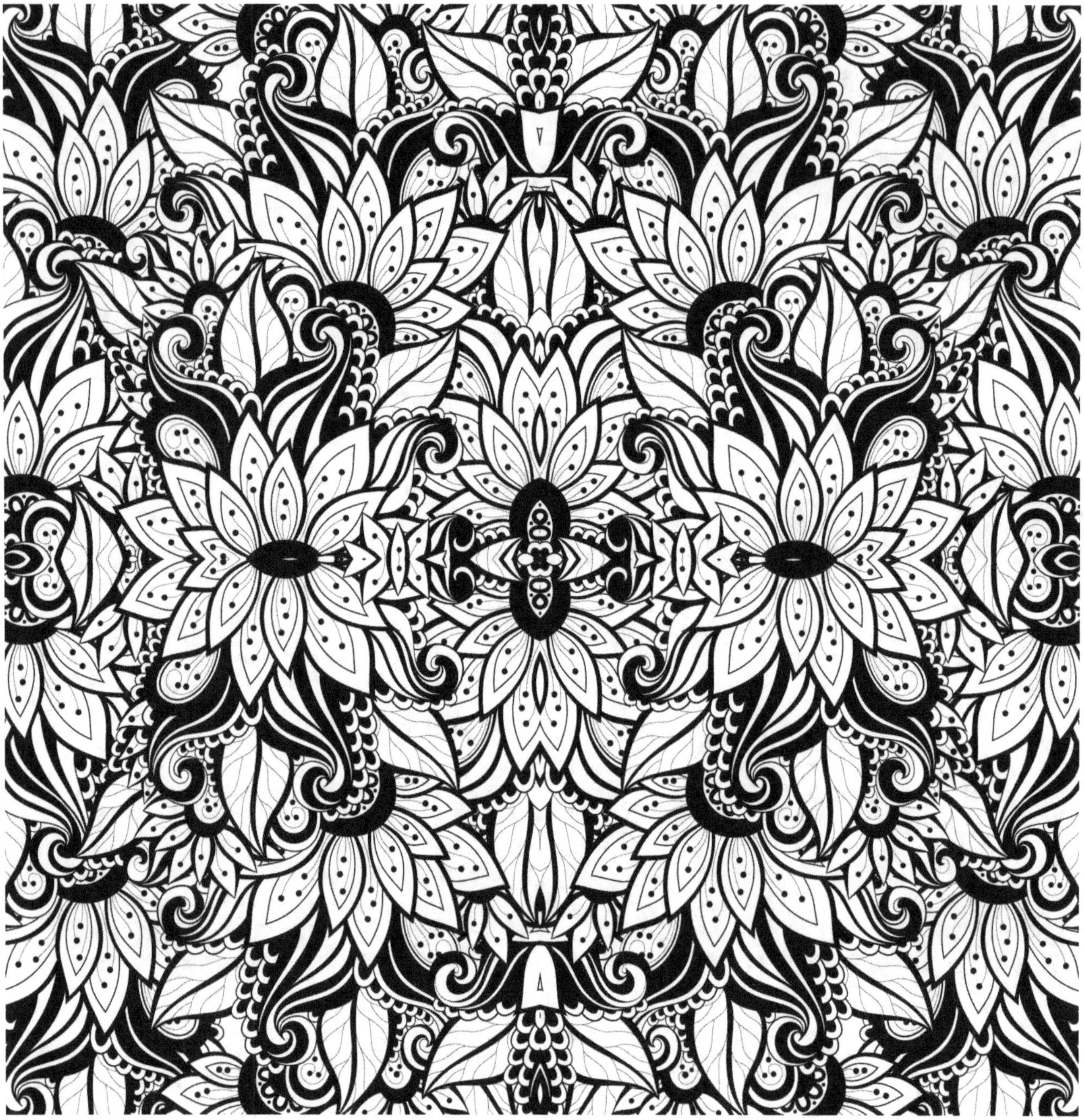

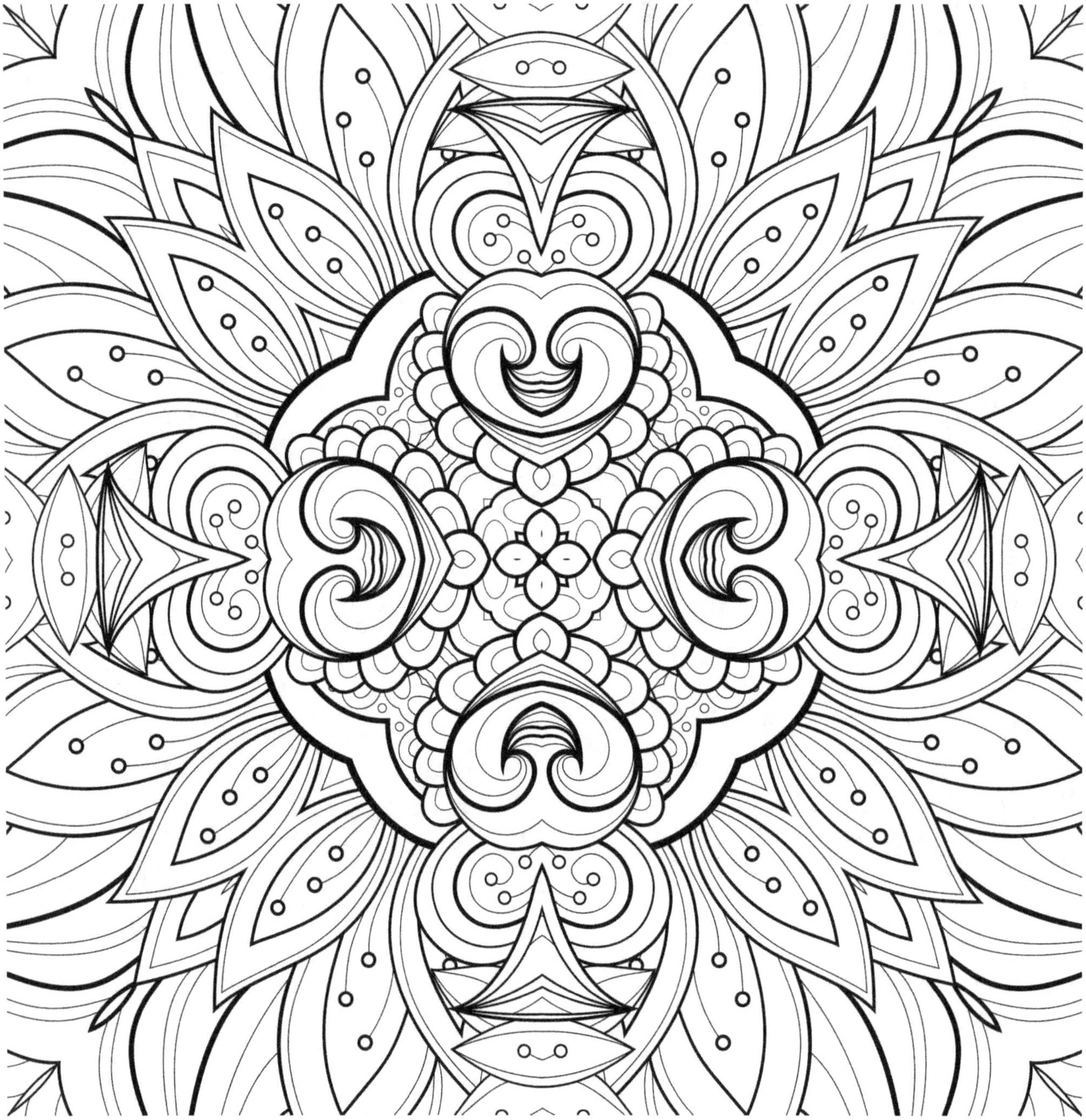

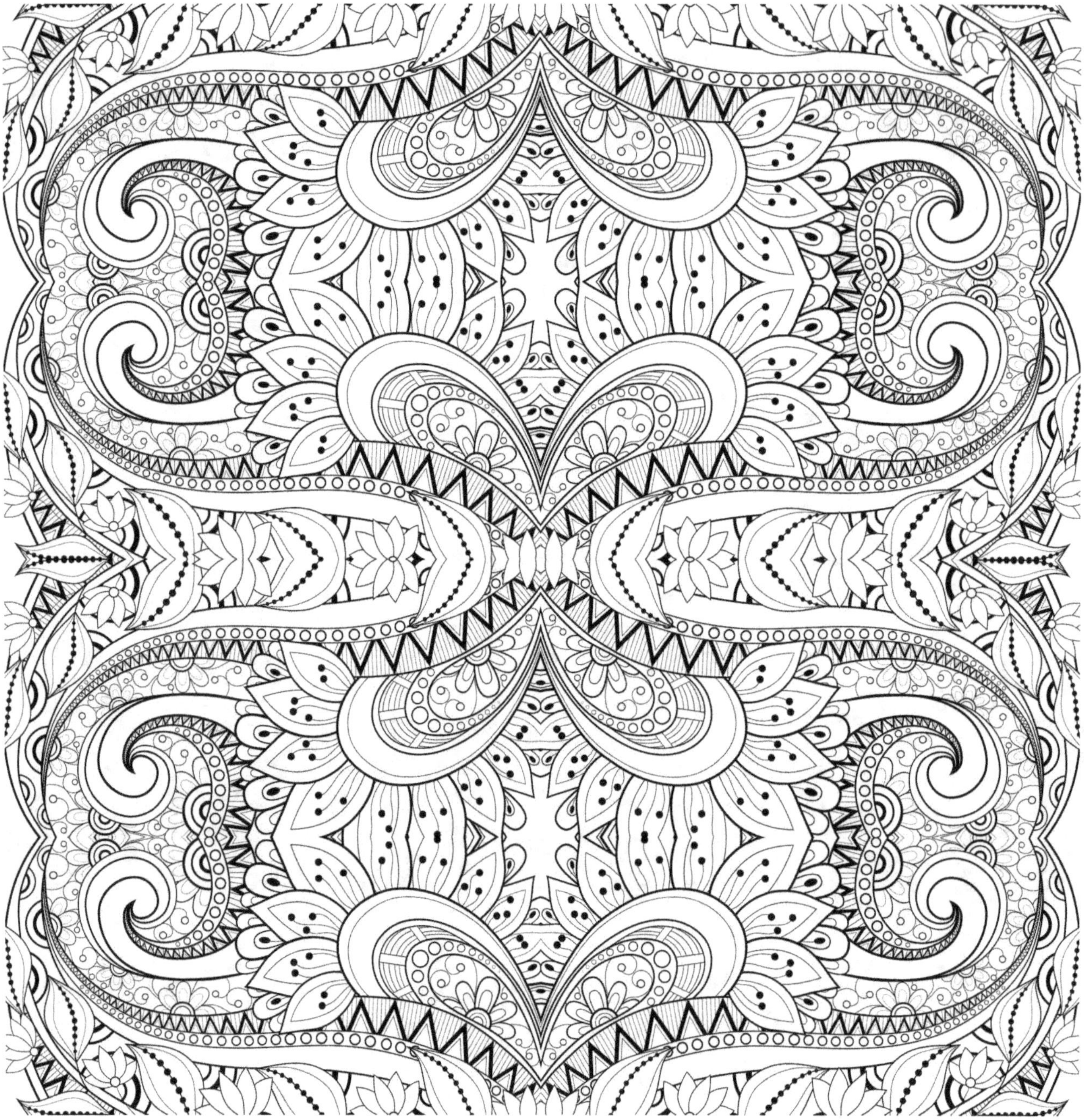

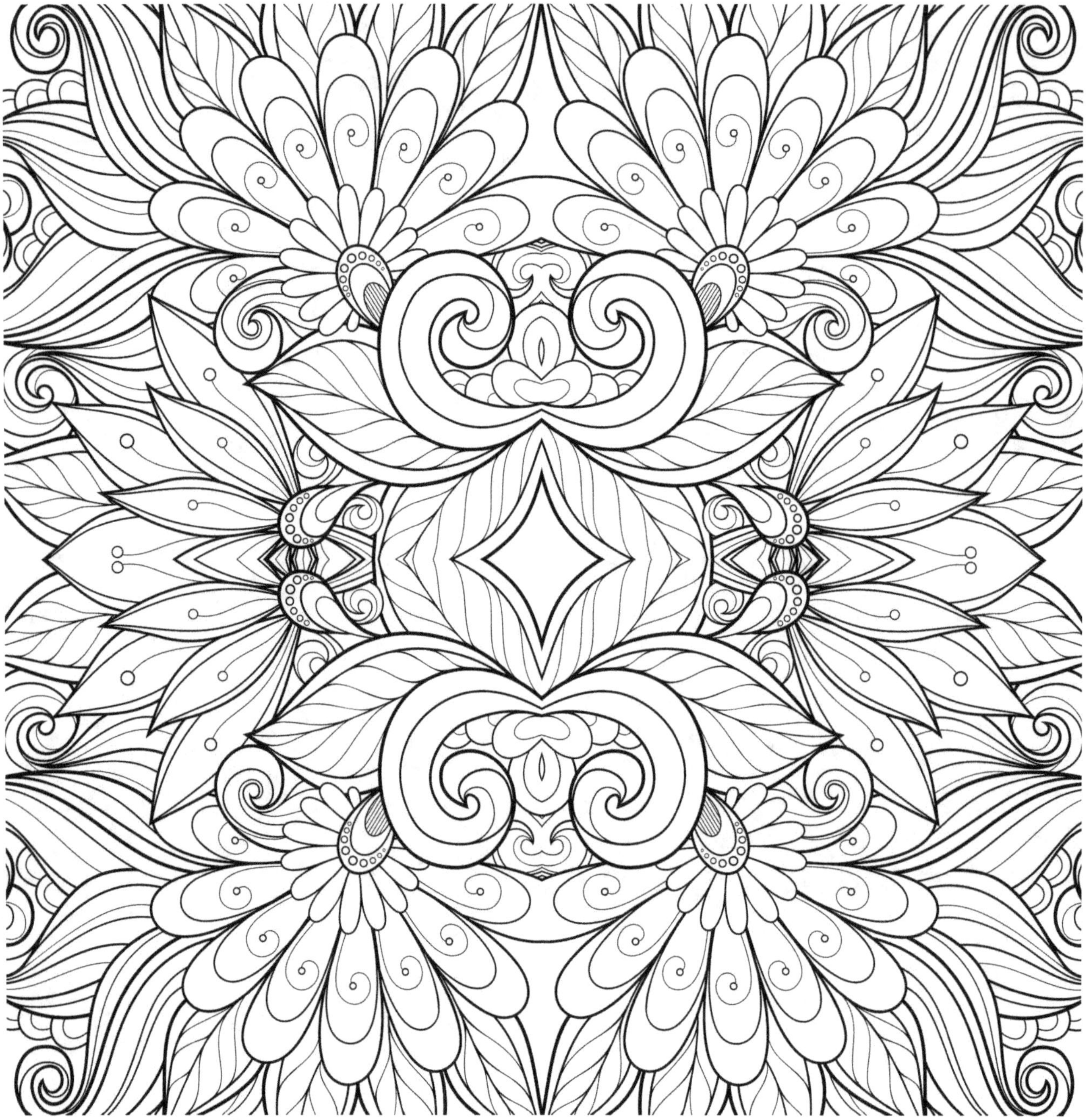

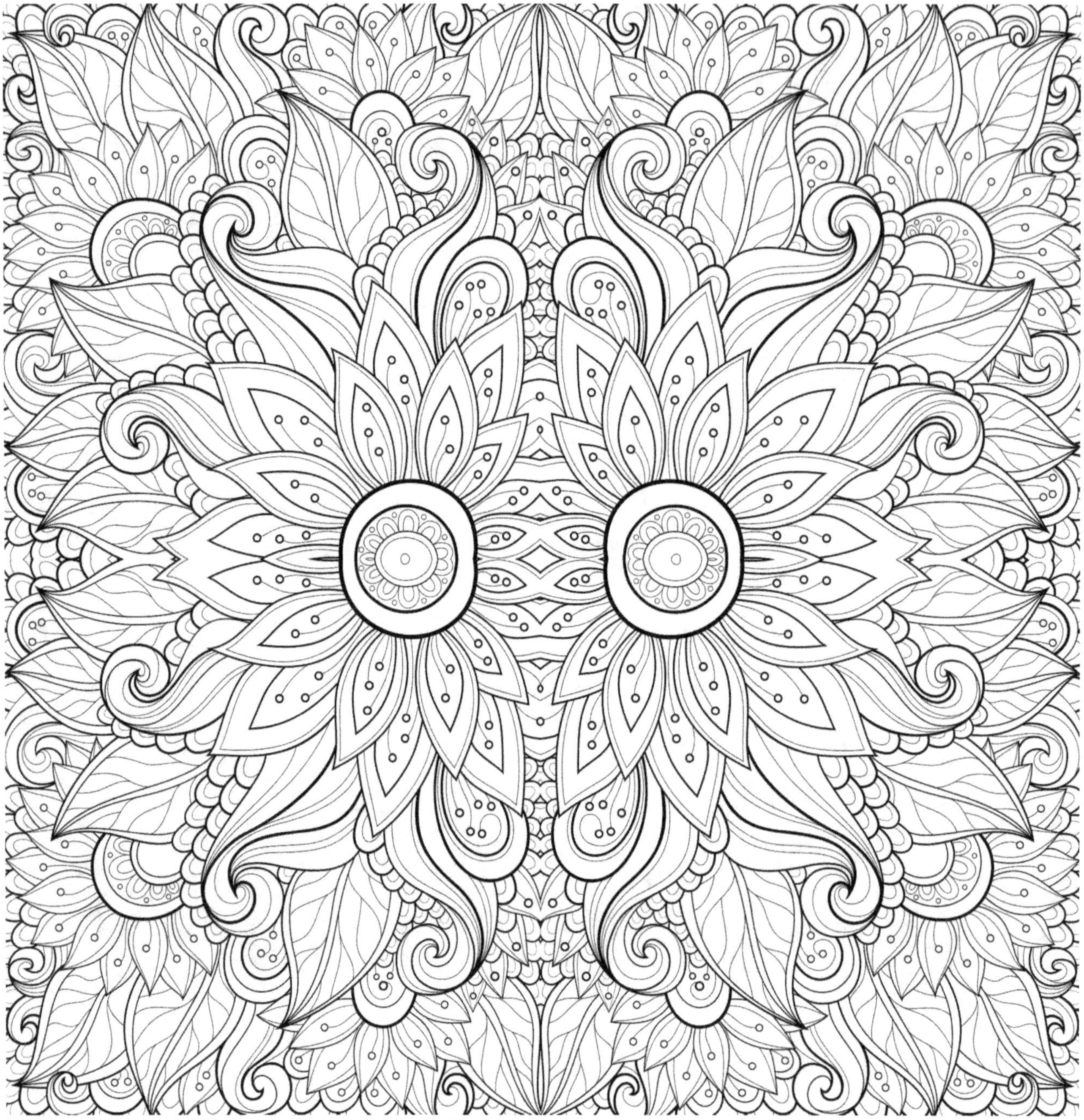

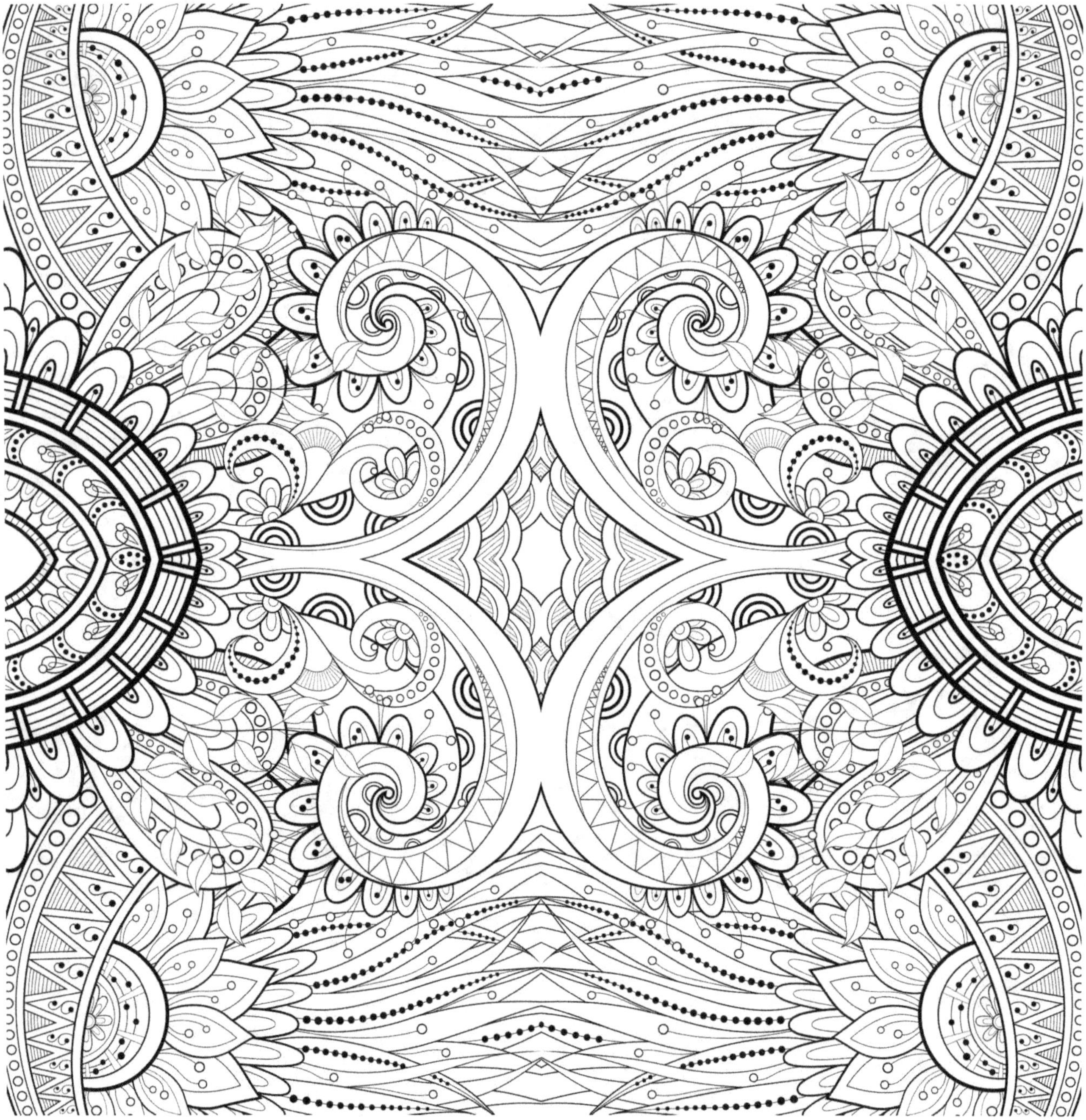

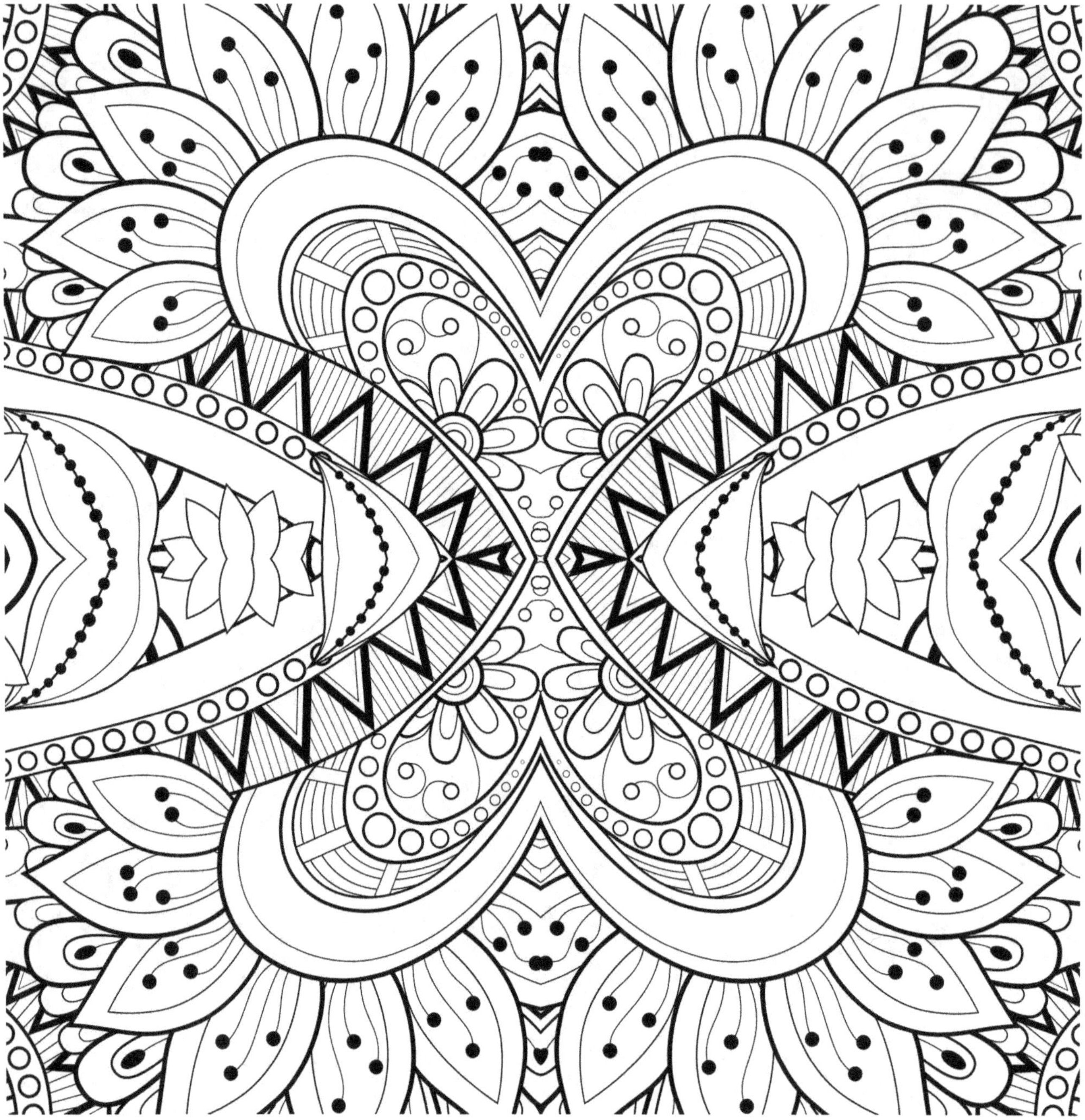

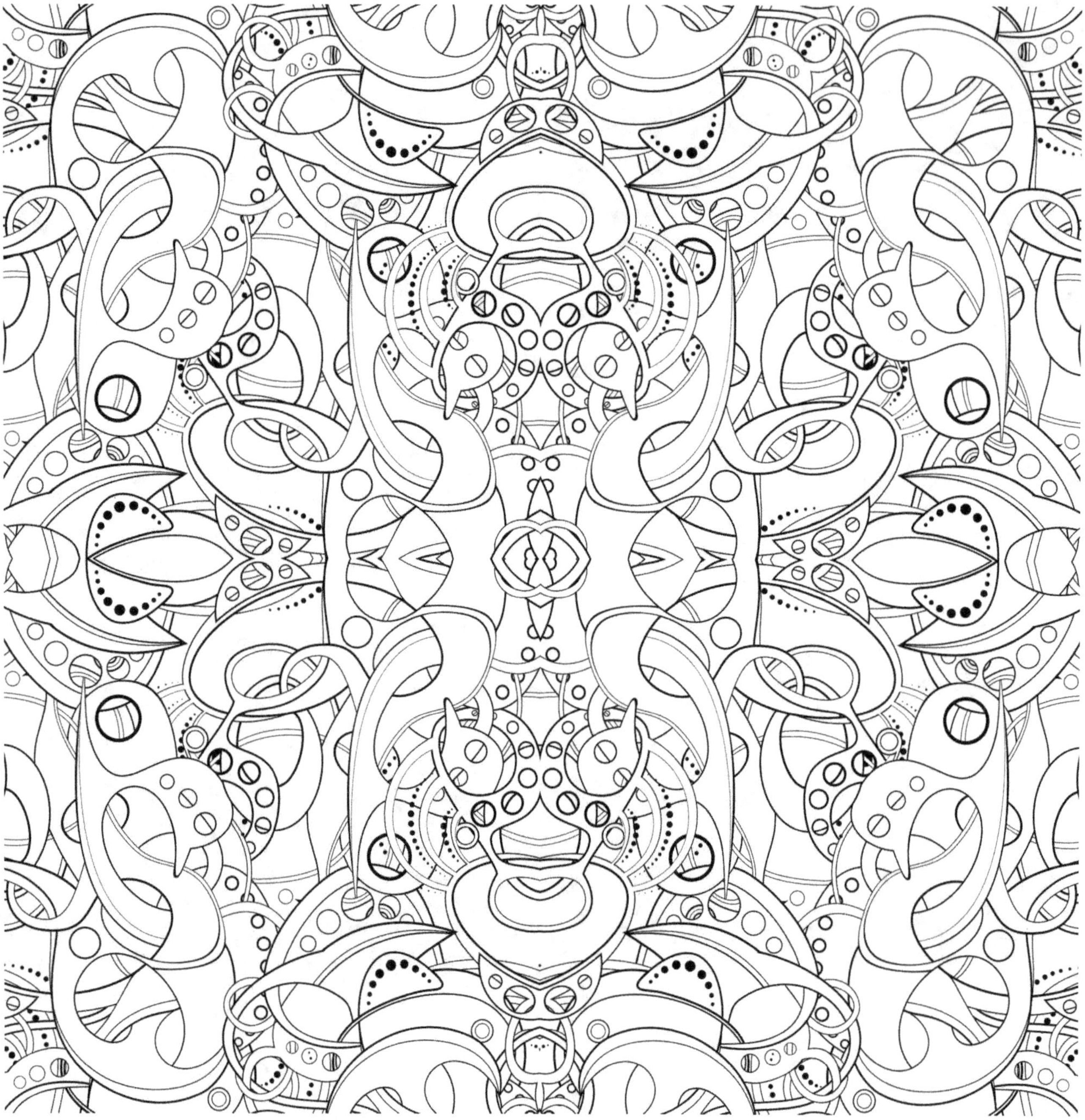

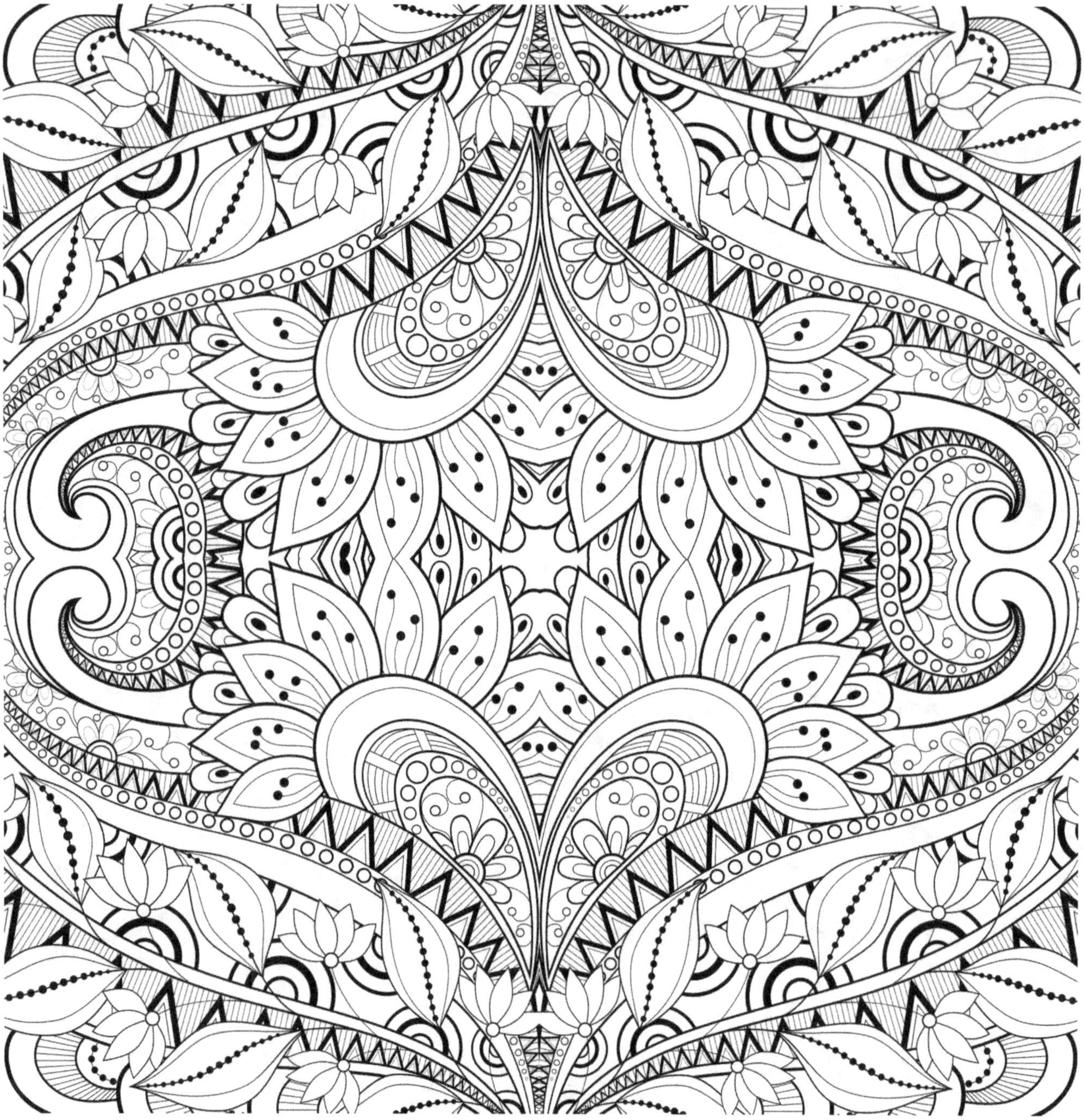

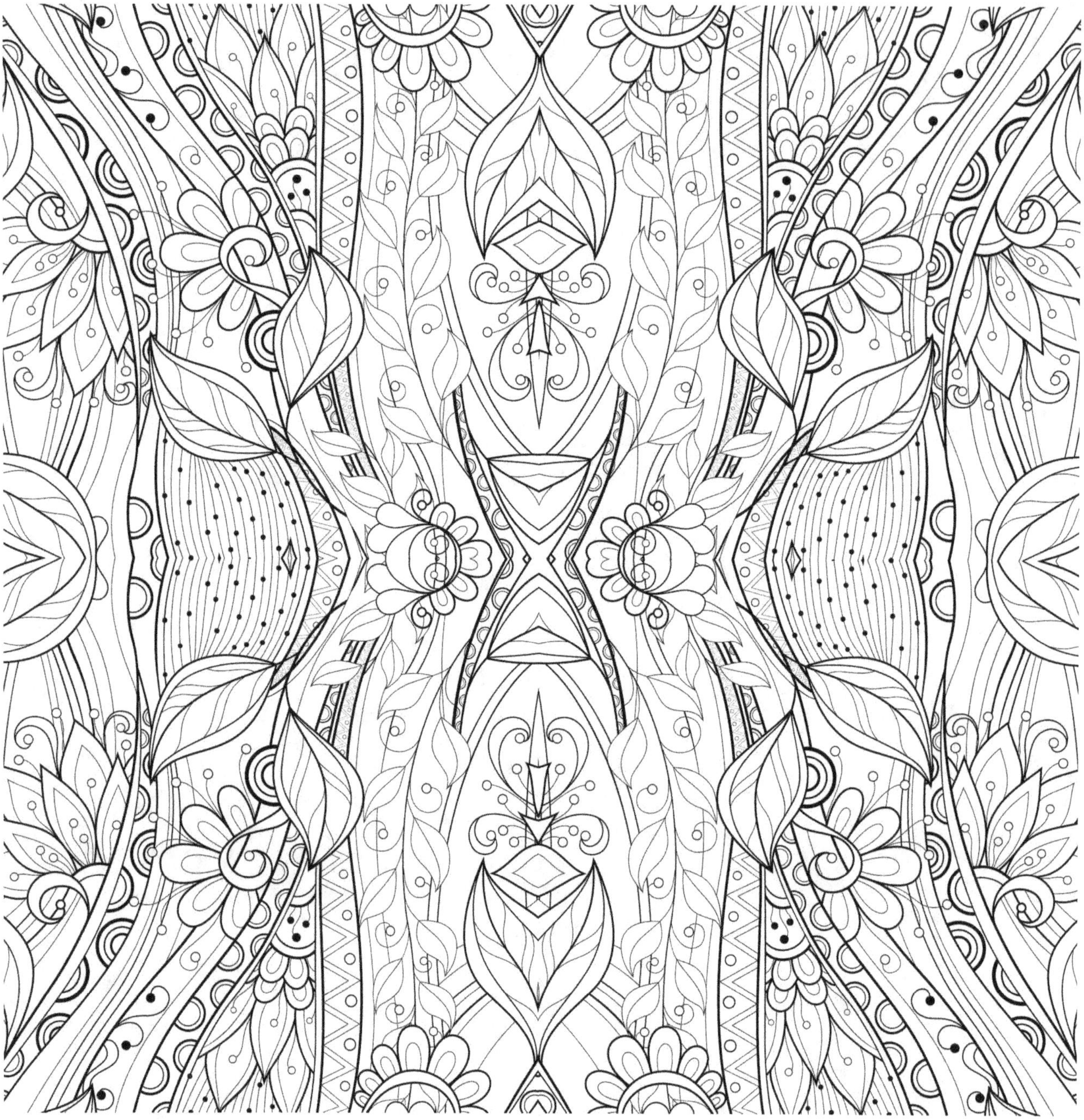

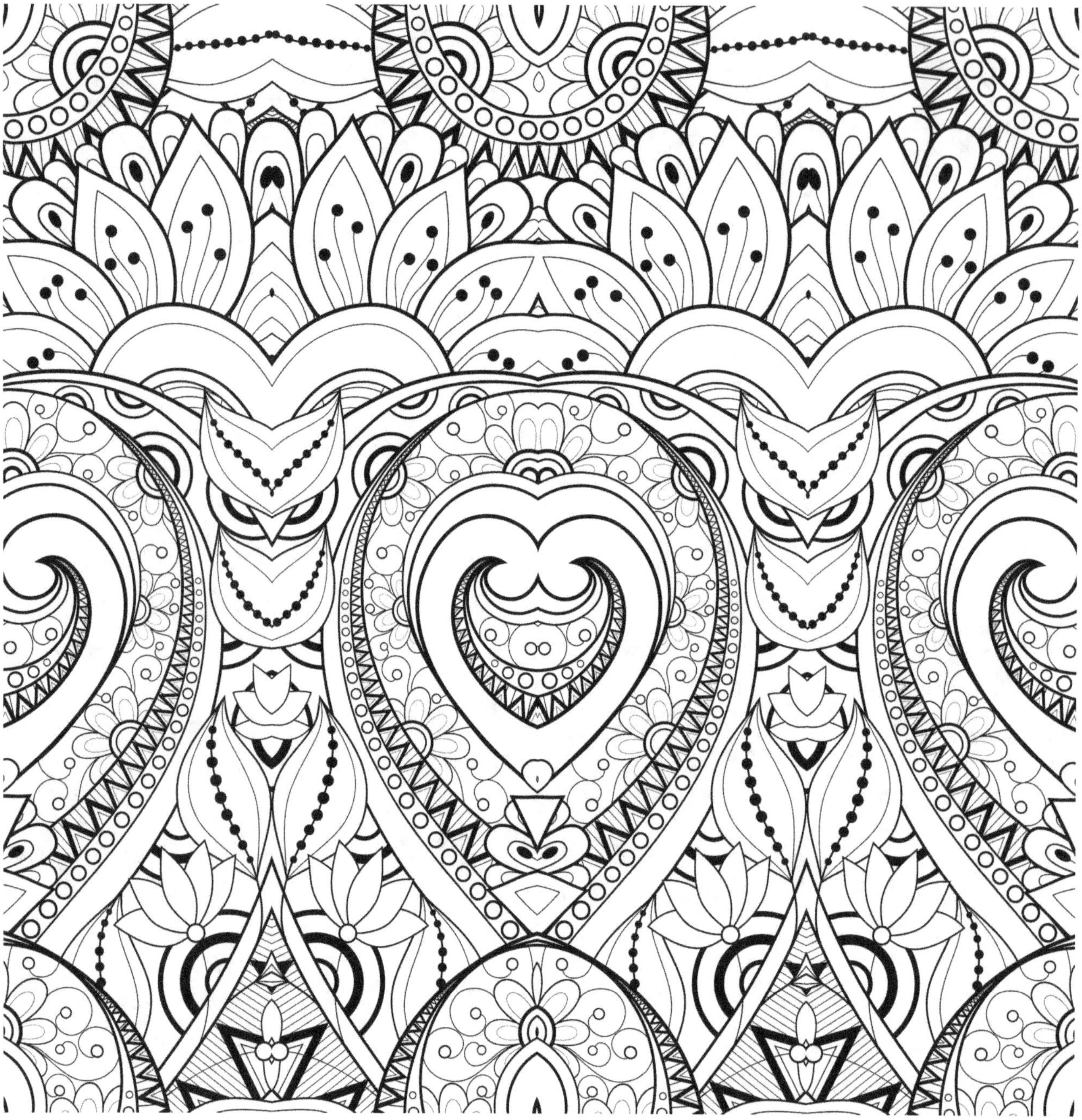

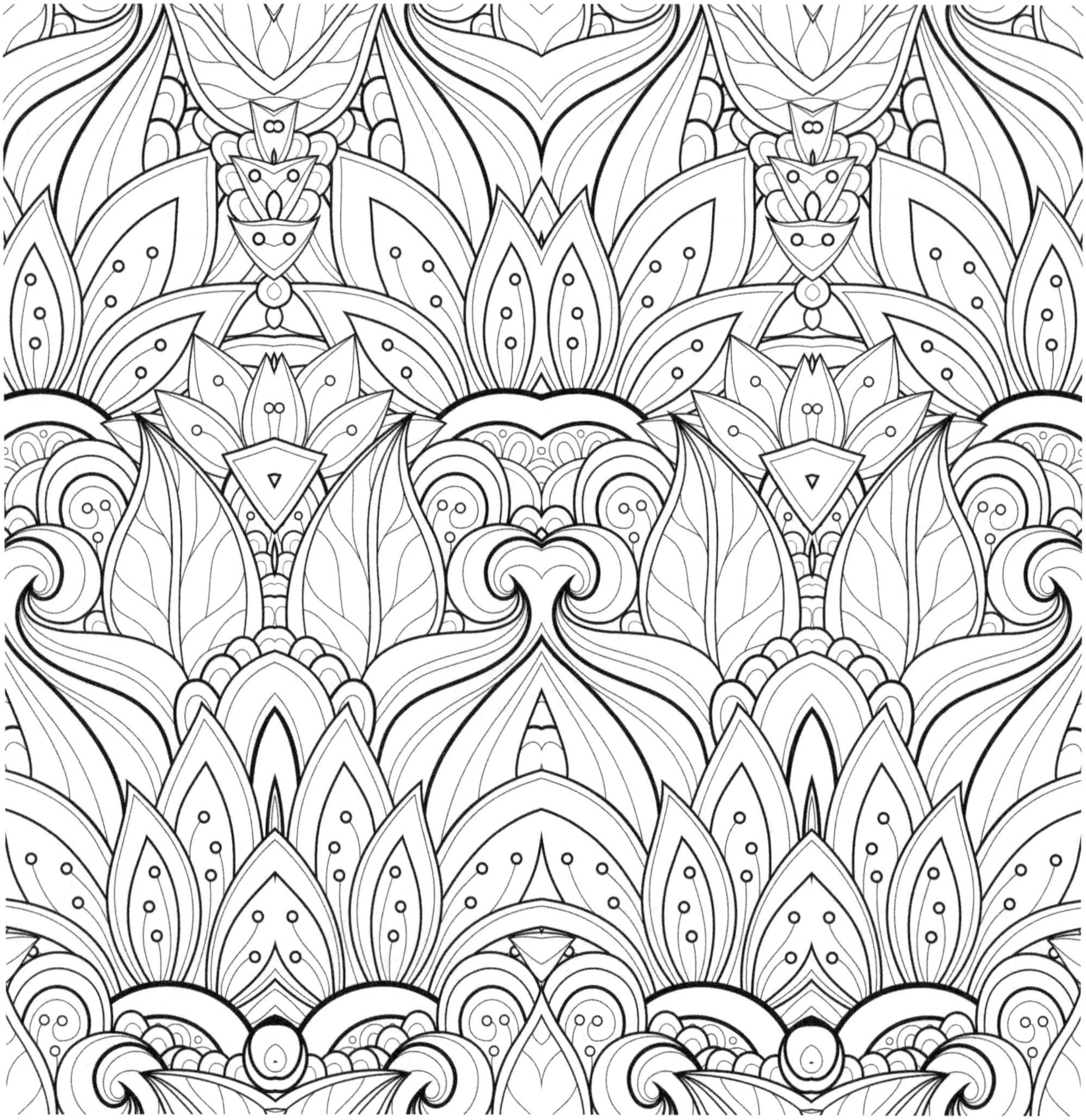

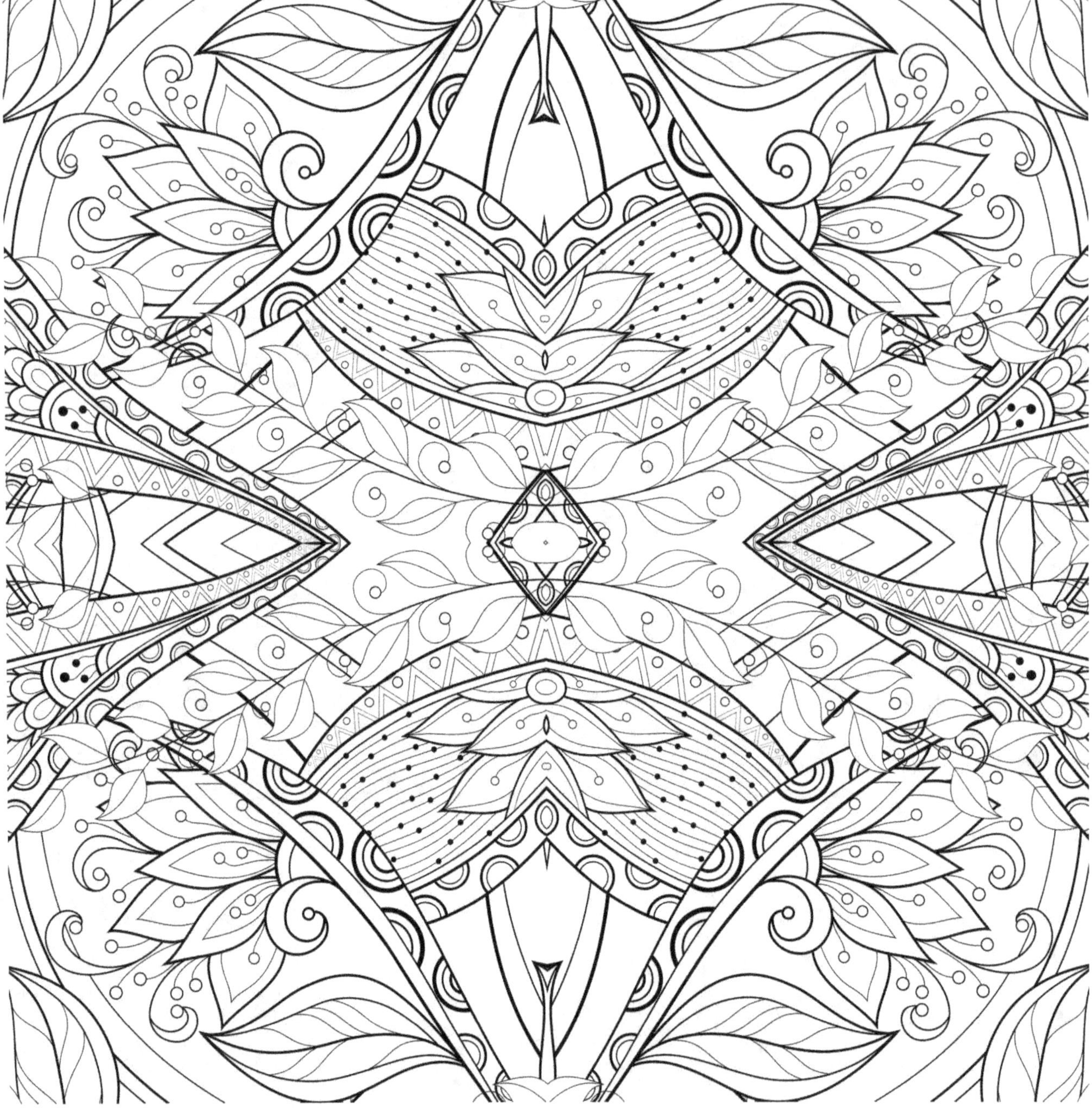

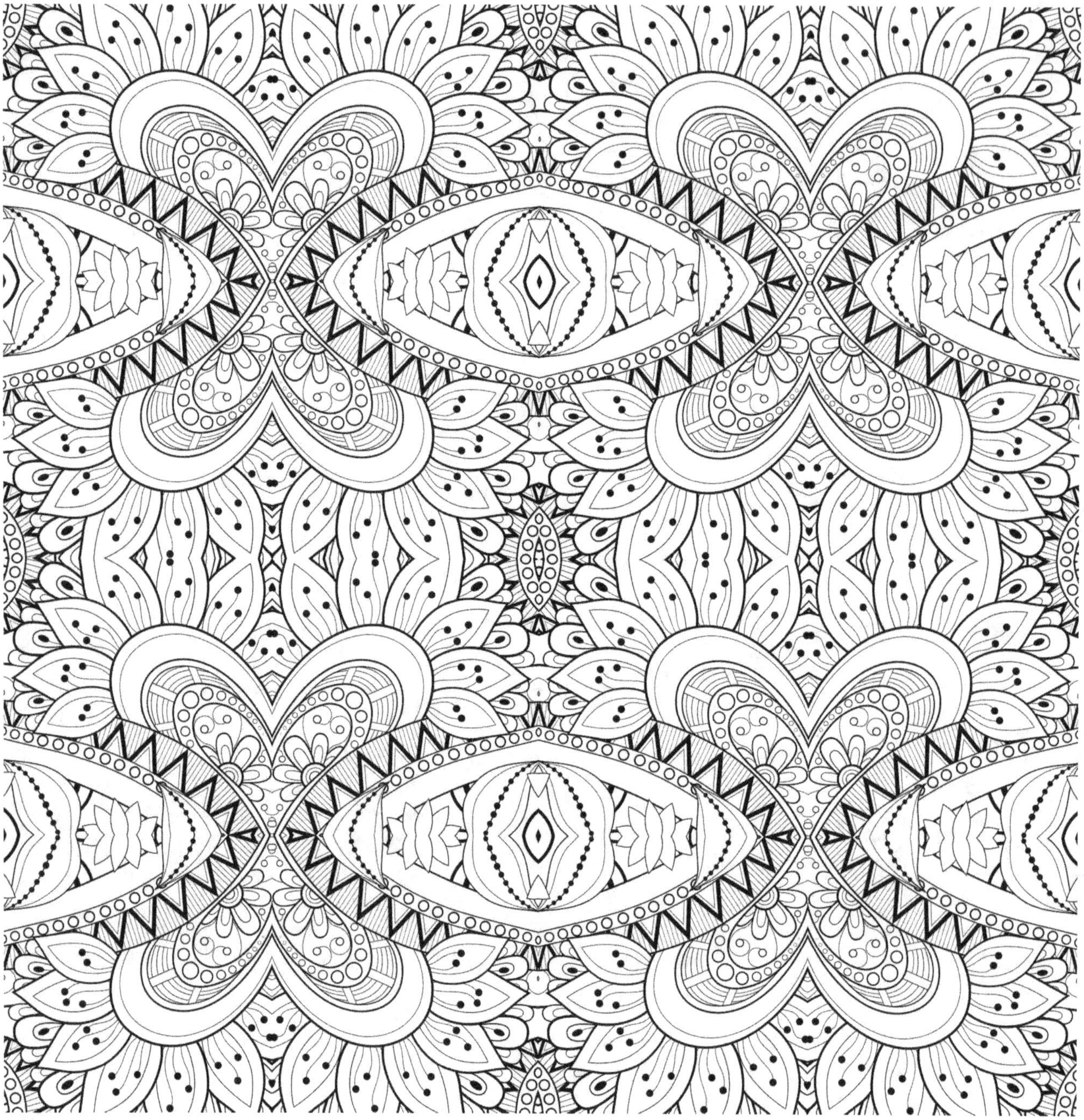

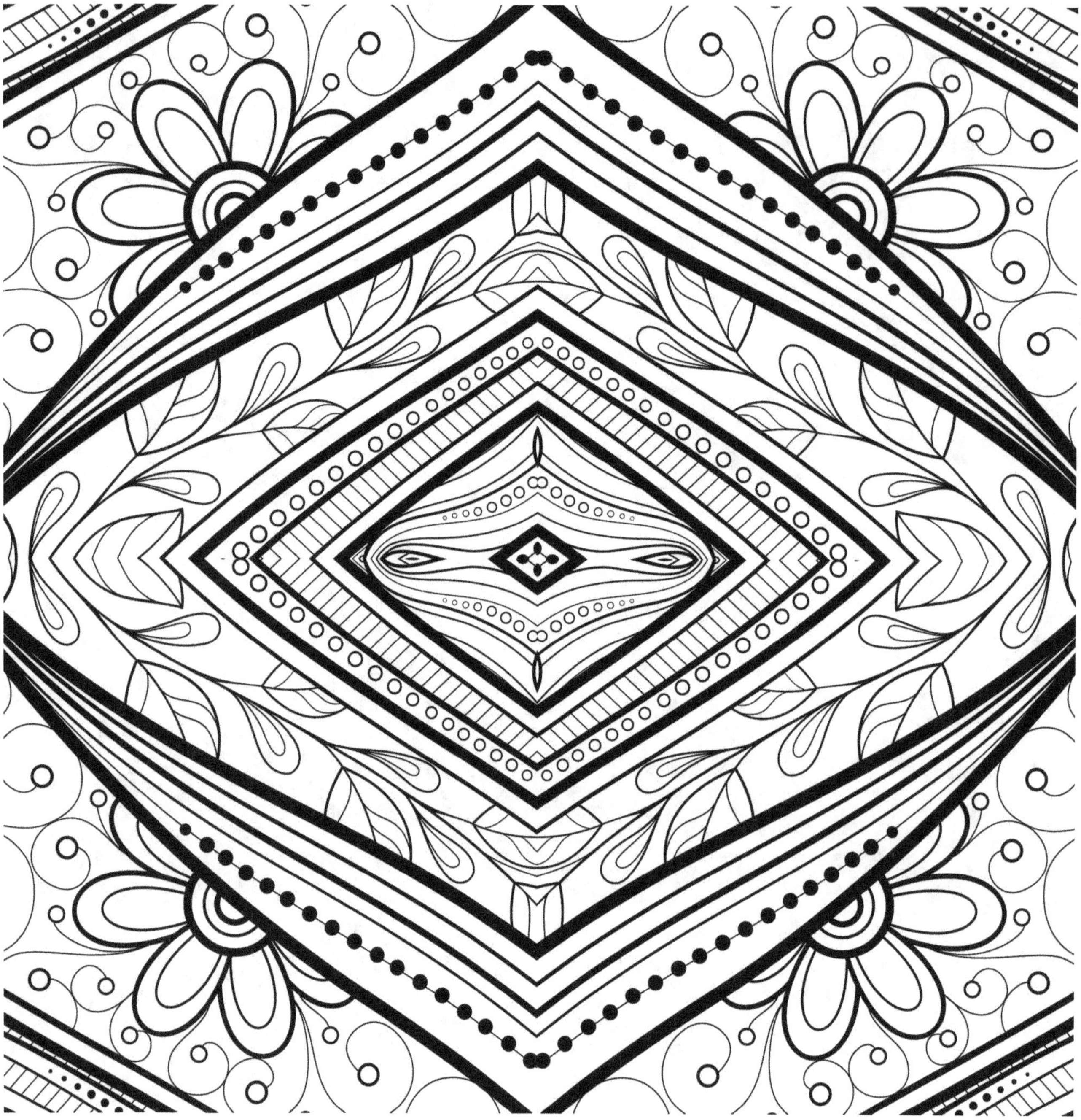

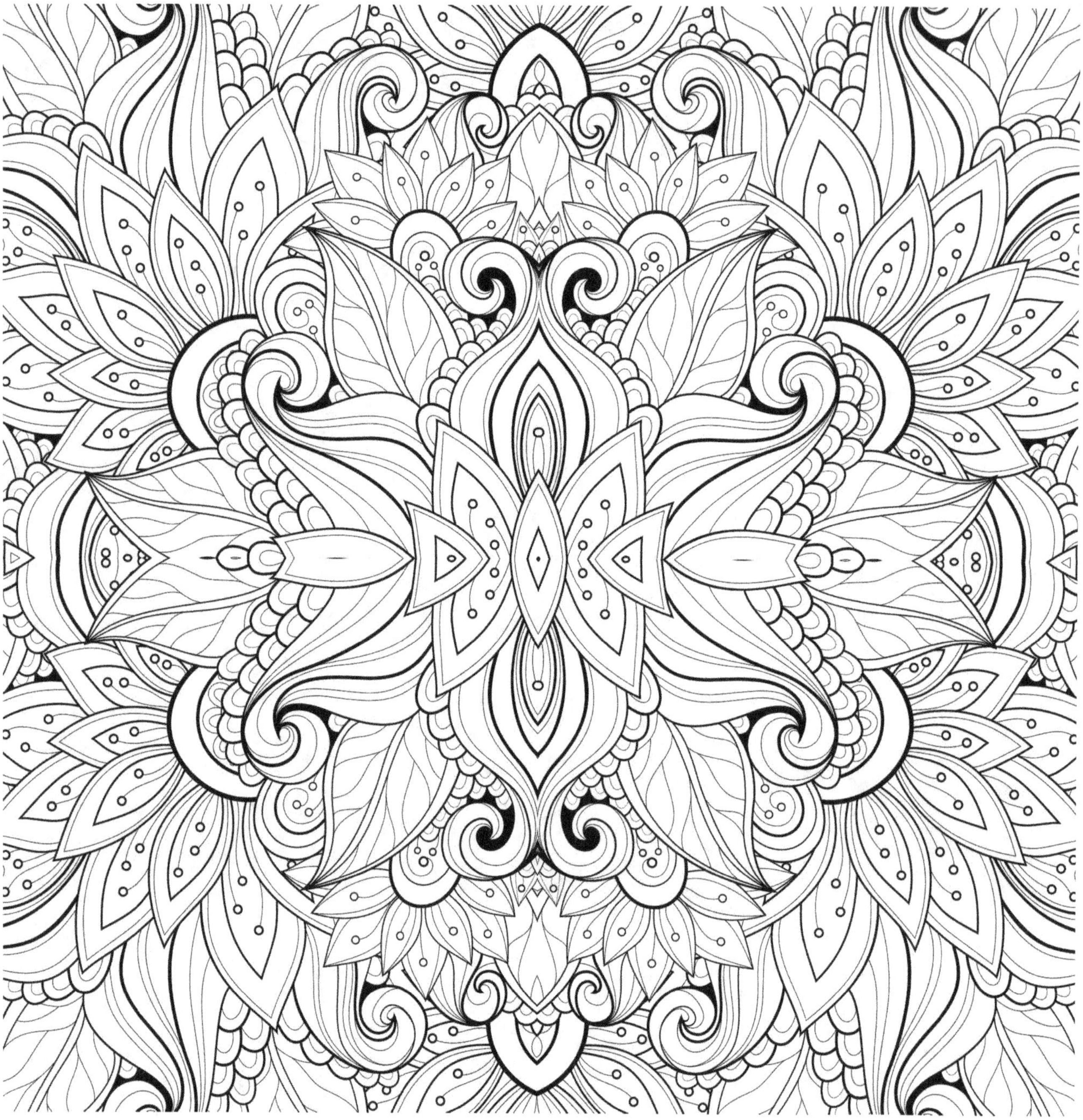

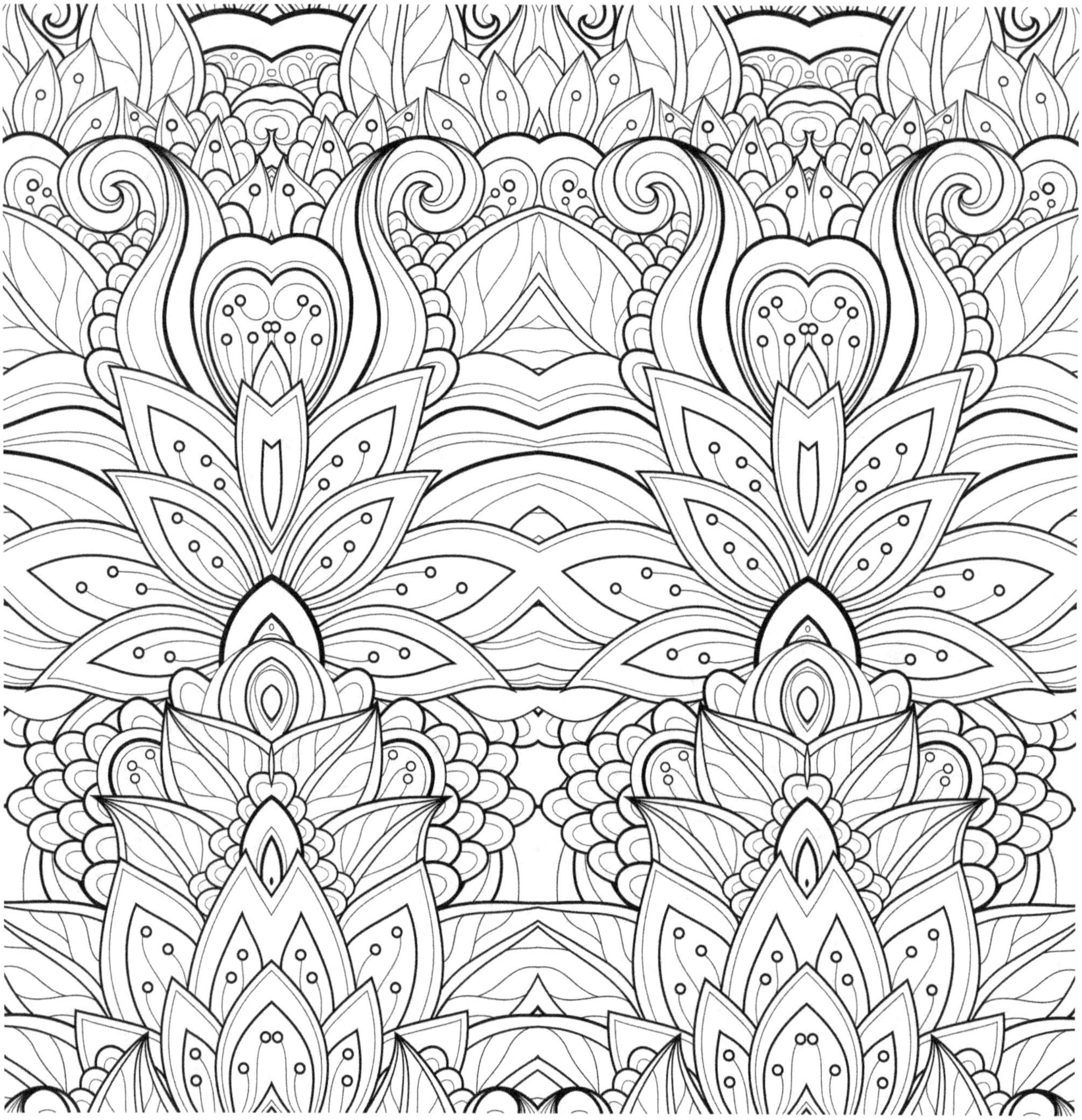

Hope you enjoy this coloring book.

Thank you.

www.ingramcontent.com/pod-product-compliance
Lightning Source LLC
Chambersburg PA
CBHW080835180526
45168CB00006B/2698
* 9 7 8 1 5 1 6 8 6 8 1 2 4 *